HOW TO OUTWIT THE SIX GHOSTS OF FEAR

"The devil fears nothing but a thinker
who controls his own mind."

Napoleon Hill,
Outwitting the Devil

HOW TO OUTWIT THE SIX GHOSTS OF FEAR

END SELF-SABOTAGE AND TAKE CONTROL OF YOUR DESTINY

AN OFFICIAL PUBLICATION OF THE

NAPOLEON HILL FOUNDATION®

Published and Distributed by
SOUND WISDOM
PO Box 310
Shippensburg, PA 17257-0310
717-530-2122

info@soundwisdom.com

www.soundwisdom.com

ISBN 13 TP: 978-1-64095-612-4

ISBN 13 eBook: 978-1-64095-613-1

For Worldwide Distribution, Printed in the USA

1 2 3 4 5 6 / 29 28 27 26

CONTENTS

FOREWORD

Napoleon Hill is the author of *Think and Grow Rich* (over 100 million copies sold!), *Master Key to Riches,* and other best-selling books. He is also the creator of the American Philosophy of Individual Achievement. His discussion on "going the extra mile" has made hundreds of thousands of wealthy men and women worldwide who have taken the time to put his wisdom into practice in their lives.

Every person needs a philosophy of life, and in Dr. Hill's books you will find the principles to guide you and sustain you in whatever work you have chosen. His philosophy does not conflict in any way with your religion or your political beliefs—but rather augments and amplifies them.

Although written a few decades ago, the wisdom, advice, humor, and proven-successful strategies are just as relevant now as they were then—in fact, even more so.

Fear is the invisible enemy that robs people of their dreams, decisions, and destiny. In *How to Outwit the Six Ghosts of Fear,* legendary success thinker Napoleon Hill reveals the six universal fears that haunt our lives—fear of poverty, criticism, ill health, loss of love, old age, and death—and shows you how to defeat them once and for all.

Drawn from Hill's groundbreaking work *Think and Grow Rich*, this standalone explorative guide offers timeless wisdom, practical steps, and deep psychological insight into the fear-driven thoughts and habits that sabotage success.

Throughout the chapters, you will discover:

- How indecision and doubt lead to fear—and how to interrupt the cycle.
- A detailed analysis of the six most common fears and how they control your actions.
- Powerful self-analysis questions to uncover and confront your own limiting beliefs.
- How to build immunity to negative influences and reclaim control of your thoughts.
- The one thing you do control—your mind—and how it determines your destiny.

"The only thing you can control is your mind." —Napoleon Hill

If you're ready to conquer fear and unlock the power of your mind, *How to Outwit the Six Ghosts of Fear* is your ultimate guide to personal power, resilience, success and proven-powerful approaches to living your best life—*fearlessly.*

We at the Napoleon Hill Foundation hope this book will inspire you to look into Napoleon Hill's original books that delve more deeply into matters of personal achievement, helping you reach that point in life when all of your plans have been fulfilled and you achieve every goal.

Don M. Green
Chief Executive Officer and Executive Director
Napoleon Hill Foundation

Preface

OUTWITTING FEAR GHOSTS

Take inventory of yourself to find out how many of the "ghosts" are standing in your way.

First and foremost, let me tell you that temporary, fleeting fear is a very important and quite normal function of the human mind. The fleeting fear of being hit as we cross the street serves to make us cautious—it protects our life—by momentarily forcing our attention on the problem of getting across safely. Thus, fear teaches us caution, but the fear is forgotten as soon as we have safely crossed.

The second important purpose of fear is to mobilize the body in defense of our life against a threatening situation. Consider for a moment the early primitive sitting, warmed by the fire in the gathering dusk, and enjoying a meal prepared during the day. Certainly, this person was at peace with the world, and the toils of the day were forgotten. Yet at this moment, a twig cracked in the forest—a sign of danger. An enemy is near. Fear alerts the senses and action results.

Frequently fear is no longer a reaction to a specific danger—now it is more a learned habit of response, a pattern of thinking that is defeating your quest for happiness and effective living.

Seek knowledge and understanding of your fear, and it will be replaced by faith.

We fear most the unknown. Seek knowledge and understanding of your fear, and it will be replaced by faith. We must cultivate and nurture a positive mental attitude to achieve that smooth, effectively functioning mind-body we seek.

You can replace ghostly, lurking fears with self-understanding and faith in yourself. To do this, we will examine the mechanism of fear and its relation to body functions.

But before you can put any portion of this philosophy into successful use, your mind must be prepared to receive it. The preparation is not difficult. It begins with study, analysis, and understanding the three enemies you have to clear out of your mind—***indecision, doubt,*** and ***fear!***

Unholy Trio

The members of the unholy trio of *indecision, doubt,* and *fear,* are closely related—where one is found, the other two are close at hand.

Indecision is the seedling of *fear.* Remember this as you read. Indecision crystallizes into *doubt,* the two blend and become *fear.* The "blending" process often is slow. This is one reason why these three enemies are so dangerous. They germinate and grow without their presence being observed.

The philosophy to outwit the six ghosts of fear as a whole analyzes an unfortunate condition that has produced huge numbers of people to poverty, and it states a truth that must be understood by all who accumulate riches, whether measured in terms of money or a state of mind of far greater value than money.

The purpose of this book is to turn the spotlight of attention on the cause and the cure of the "ghosts" that haunt us off and on throughout our lives. Before we can master an enemy, we must know its name, its habits, and its place of abode. As you read, analyze yourself carefully, and determine which, if any, of the six common fears have attached themselves to you.

Do not be deceived by the habits of these subtle ghostly enemies. Sometimes they remain hidden in the subconscious mind where they are difficult to locate, and still more difficult to eliminate. But always remember that each *can* be overcome and defeated.

Six Basic Fears

There are six basic fears that every human suffers from at one time or another. Most people are fortunate if they do not suffer from the entire six. Named in the order of their most common appearance. The fear of:

1. **Poverty**
2. **Criticism**
3. **Ill Health**
4. **Loss of Love**
5. **Old Age**
6. **Death**

All other fears are of minor importance and can be grouped under these six headings.

We are here laying the foundation for the presentation of a fact of great importance to those who do not understand why some people appear to be "lucky" while others of equal or greater ability, training, experience, and brain capacity, seem destined to ride with misfortune. This fact may be explained by the statement that every human being has the ability to completely control his own mind—and with this control, obviously, every person may open their mind to the tramp thought impulses that are being released by other brains, or close the doors tightly and admit only thought impulses of his or her own choice.

Nature has endowed humans with absolute control over only one thing—our thoughts. This fact, coupled with the additional fact that everything humankind creates begins in the form of a thought, leads us to the principle by which the ghosts of fear may be mastered.

Chapter 1

POVERTY

Fearing poverty is a state of mind—and is sufficient to destroy your chances of achievement.

Your State of Mind

Fearing poverty is a state of mind, nothing else! But this fear is sufficient to destroy our chances of achievement in any undertaking, a truth that became painfully evident during the Great Depression and in ebbs and tides during subsequent economic fluctuations.

The fear of poverty:

- Paralyzes the faculty of reason
- Destroys the faculty of imagination
- Kills off self-reliance
- Undermines enthusiasm
- Discourages initiative
- Leads to uncertainty of purpose
- Encourages procrastination

- Wipes out enthusiasm
- Makes self-control an impossibility

The fear of poverty also:

- Takes the charm from your personality
- Destroys the possibility of accurate thinking
- Diverts concentration of effort and persistence
- Turns willpower into nothingness
- Destroys ambition
- Beclouds the memory
- Invites failure in every conceivable form
- Kills love and assassinates the finer emotions of the heart
- Discourages friendship and invites disaster in a hundred forms
- Leads to sleeplessness, misery, and unhappiness

And all this despite the obvious truth that we live in a nation of over-abundance of everything the heart could desire, with nothing standing between us and our desires, except the lack of a definite purpose.

If you demand riches, determine what form, and how much will be required to satisfy you. There is a road that leads to riches—it is paved with determination, focus, and steady work. If you neglect to start down that road, or stop before you arrive, no one will be to blame, but you. This responsibility is yours. No alibi will save you from accepting the responsibility if you fail or refuse to demand riches of life, because the acceptance calls for only one thing—incidentally, the only thing you can control—your state of mind. A state of mind is something you create and control. It cannot be purchased, it must be created.

Nothing stands between you and your desires, except the lack of a definite purpose.

Most Destructive Ghost

The fear of poverty ghost is, without a doubt, the most destructive of the six basic fears. It has been placed at the head of the list, because it is the most difficult to master. Considerable courage is required to state the truth about the origin of this fear, and still greater courage to accept the truth after it has been stated. The fear of poverty actually grew out of humanity's inherited tendency to prey upon other people economically.

Nearly all animals lower than humans are motivated by instinct. Their capacity to "think" is limited, therefore, they prey upon one another physically. Humankind, with our superior sense of intuition, with the capacity to think and to reason, does not eat our compadres bodily, we get more satisfaction out of "eating" them financially. We are so avaricious that every conceivable law has been passed to safeguard us from other people's greed.

Of all the ages of the world, of which we know anything, the age in which we live seems to be outstanding because of our money-madness. A man is considered less than the dust of the earth unless he can display a fat bank account. And if he has money—never mind how he acquired it—he is considered a "big shot." He is above the law, he rules in politics, he dominates in business, and the whole world around him bows in respect when he passes.

On the other hand, nothing brings so much suffering and humility as poverty. Only those who have experienced poverty understand the full meaning of this.

It is no wonder that most people fear living in poverty. So eager are some of us to possess wealth that we will acquire it in whatever manner possible—through legal methods or through other methods if necessary or expedient.

There can be no compromise between *poverty* and *riches.* Two roads lead to poverty or riches and travel in opposite directions. If you want riches, you must refuse to accept any circumstance that leads to poverty. (The word "riches" is here used in its broadest sense, meaning financial, spiritual, mental, and material estates.)

The starting point of the path that leads to riches is *desire.* (In Chapter 2 of my book *Today—You Can Think and Grow Rich,* there are full instructions for the proper use of desire.) This chapter examines the poverty ghost and will prepare your mind to make practical use of desire.

Desire is the starting point for all accomplishments.

A long while ago, a great warrior had to make a decision that ensured his success on the battlefield. He was about to send his armies against a powerful foe whose men outnumbered his. He loaded his soldiers into boats, sailed to the enemy's country, and unloaded the soldiers and equipment. Then he gave the order to burn the ships that had carried them. Addressing his men before the first battle, he said, "You see the boats going up in smoke. That means we cannot leave these shores alive unless we win! We now have no choice—we win or we perish!"

They won.

Everyone who wins in any undertaking must be willing to burn the ships and cut all sources of retreat. That is the only way you can be sure of maintaining the state of mind known as a "burning desire" to win. It is essential to success.

Here, then, is the place to give yourself a challenge. Here is the point where you can turn prophet and foretell, accurately, what the future holds in store for you. If, after reading this chapter, you are willing to accept poverty, you may as well make up your mind to receive poverty. This is one decision you cannot avoid.

Self-Analysis

Self-analysis may disclose weaknesses we do not like to acknowledge. This form of examination is essential for all who demand of life more than mediocrity and poverty. Remember as you check yourself point by point—you are both the judge and the jury, the prosecuting attorney and the attorney for the defense, you are the plaintiff and the defendant, and you are on trial. Face the facts squarely.

Ask yourself definite questions and demand direct replies. When the examination is over, you will know more about yourself. If you do not feel that you can be an impartial judge in this self-examination, call upon someone who knows you well to serve as judge while you cross-examine yourself. You are after the truth. Get it no matter the cost, even though it may temporarily embarrass you!

The majority of people, if asked what they fear most, would reply, "I fear nothing." The reply would be inaccurate, because few people realize that they are bound, handicapped, whipped spiritually and physically through some form of fear. So subtle and deeply seated is the ghostly emotion of fear that we may go through life burdened with it, never recognizing its presence.

Only a courageous analysis will disclose the presence of this universal enemy. When you begin such an analysis, search deeply into your character. The following is a list of symptoms to look for:

Self-examination is essential for all who demand more of life than mediocrity and poverty.

Fear of Poverty Symptoms

Indifference

Commonly expressed through lack of ambition; willingness to tolerate poverty; acceptance of whatever compensation life may offer without protest; mental and physical laziness; lack of initiative, imagination, enthusiasm, and self-control.

Indecision

The habit of permitting others to do your thinking. Satisfied with sitting "on the fence."

Doubt

Generally expressed through alibis and excuses designed to cover up, explain away, or apologize for failures; sometimes expressed in the form of envy of those who are successful, or by criticizing them.

Worry

Usually expressed by finding fault with others, a tendency to spend beyond your income, neglect of personal appearance, scowling and frowning; intemperance in the use of alcoholic drink, sometimes through the use of narcotics; nervousness, lack of poise, self-consciousness, and lack of self-reliance.

Overcautious

The habit of looking for the negative side of every circumstance, thinking and talking of possible failure instead of concentrating on how to succeed. Knowing all the roads to disaster, but never searching for the plans to avoid failure. Waiting for "the right time" to begin putting ideas and plans into action, until the waiting becomes a permanent habit. Remembering those who have failed, and forgetting those who have succeeded. Seeing the hole in the doughnut, but overlooking the doughnut. Pessimism, leading to indigestion, poor elimination, autointoxication, bad breath, and bad disposition.

Procrastination

The habit of putting off until tomorrow what should have been done last year. Spending enough time in creating alibis and excuses to have done the job. This symptom is closely related to overcaution, doubt, and worry. Refusal to accept responsibility when it can be avoided. Willingness to compromise rather than put up a stiff fight. Compromising with difficulties instead of harnessing and using them as stepping stones to advancement. Bargaining with life for a penny, instead of demanding prosperity, opulence, riches, contentment and happiness.

Planning what to do if and when overtaken by failure—instead of burning all bridges and making retreat impossible. Weakness of, and often total lack of self-confidence, definiteness of purpose, self-control, initiative, enthusiasm, ambition, thrift, and sound reasoning ability. Expecting poverty instead of demanding riches. Associating with those who accept poverty instead of seeking the company of those who demand and receive riches.

Because it is true that all thought has a tendency to clothe itself in its physical equivalent (and this is true beyond any reasonable room for doubt), it is equally true that thought impulses of fear and poverty *cannot* be translated into terms of courage and financial gain.

United States citizens began to focus their thoughts on poverty following the Wall Street crash of 1929. Slowly but surely, that "mass thought" was crystallized into its physical equivalent, which was and is known as "depression." This had to happen, it is in conformity with the laws of Nature.

Habitual thoughts of fear and poverty CANNOT be translated into courage and financial gain.

Money Talks

Some will ask, "Why did you write a book about money? Why measure riches in dollars, alone?" Some will believe, and rightly so, that there are other forms of riches more desirable than money. Yes, there are riches that cannot be measured in terms of dollars, but there are millions of people who will say, "Give me all the money I need, and I will find everything else I want."

The major reason why I wrote books on how to get money is the fact that the world has passed through experiences that left millions of men and women paralyzed because of the fear of poverty ghost.

Poverty is the result of a negative condition of the mind, which practically every living person experiences at one time or another. It is the first and the most disastrous of the basic fears, but it is only a state of mind; and like the other fears, it is subject to the control of each individual.

Most Accept Poverty as Inescapable

The fact that a major portion of all people are born in surroundings of poverty, accept it as inescapable, and go with it all though their lives, indicates how potent a factor it is in the lives of people. It may well be that poverty is one of the testing devices the Creator uses to separate the weak from the strong? For it is a notable fact that those who master poverty become

Those who master poverty become rich not only in material things, but also rich and often wise in spiritual values as well.

rich not only in material things, but also rich and often wise in spiritual values as well.

I have observed that people who have mastered poverty invariably have a keen sense of faith in their ability to master practically everything else that stands in the way of their progress; while those who have accepted poverty as inescapable show signs of weakness in many other directions.

In no case have I known anyone who had accepted poverty as unavoidable, who had not failed also to exercise that great gift of the power to take possession of their own mind-power (as the Creator intended all people should do).

All people go through testing periods throughout their lives, under many circumstances, that clearly disclose whether or not they have accepted and used the great gift of exclusive control over their own mind-power. And I have observed that along with this great gift from the Infinite go also definite penalties for neglect to embrace and use the gift, and definite rewards for its recognition and use.

One of the more important rewards for using the power of your mind and to control your state of mind consists in complete freedom from the entire six basic fears and all the lesser fears, with full access to the power of faith to replace fears.

The penalties for neglecting to embrace and use this great gift of controlling your mind are multitude. In addition to possibly being visited by all of the six basic fear ghosts, there are many other liabilities not included with these fears. One major penalty for failure to use your mind is the total impossibility of enjoying peace of mind.

Attaining peace of mind is to control your state of mind.

– Reflection Journal –

Use the space below to capture your insights. Be honest and detailed. Writing by hand strengthens clarity and awareness.

Prompt

- What are your thoughts about the statement: "The fear of poverty actually grew out of humanity's inherited tendency to prey upon other people economically"? If you fear being poor, how does this statement reflect your view?
- Which symptoms of poverty fear show up in your life today, and how can you replace them with decisive action?
- How often do you experience peace of mind, a calm serenity within, feeling safe and secure? Routinely? Rarely? Why?

My Reflections

Daily Affirmation

Speak this out loud, with conviction. Repetition builds belief, and belief transforms into action.

Affirmation for This Chapter

> ***"I release all thoughts of lack. I choose abundance, purpose, and peace of mind."***

- ❑ **Repeat** it **3 times aloud.**
- ❑ **Write** it here once, slowly and deliberately:

Action Step

Choose one small action you can take this week to apply what you've learned.

Chapter 2

CRITICISM

Criticism is the one form of service, of which everyone has too much.

Criticism is the basic fear of what people will say or think about them and keeps many from developing and presenting ideas that would give them independence if acted upon. Thus, fear of criticism robs people of their individuality. It undermines their self-reliance and develops an inferiority complex within.

Often the cruelest critics of everything we do, or plan to do, are our relatives. Therefore, it is necessary to caution you: Keep your definite major purpose to yourself. Do not express it before those who may seize upon it with criticism and attempt to thwart your ambition to excel your previous efforts.

Parents with good intentions, but a limited understanding of human relations, often do their children irreparable injury by criticizing them, shaming them, or making fun of them and their childhood dreams of achievement. Teasing an adolescent boy about his girl friends, and vice versa, is very definitely a dangerous practice that may lead to permanent social maladjustment in cases of a sensitive personality.

Strangely enough, criticism is one form of service that nearly everyone renders willingly, and usually without charge or invitation. Criticism is the one type of service nearly everyone is very generous with doling out.

There is, however, a very significant difference between criticism and constructive suggestions. Often an employee, an associate, or a child needs correction. Some of his or her habits may be unproductive, wasteful, or in bad taste. A well-balanced person will learn to accept constructive suggestion in the spirit in which it is given, and will not brood over mistakes of the past.

The three most obvious symptoms of the fear of criticism are:

1. A desire to keep up with the Joneses. This prompts you to try to maintain a front in competition with your neighbors, even if it causes you to spend beyond your income.

2. The habit of bragging about your achievements, either real or imaginary. It often happens that a person will cover up feelings of inferiority by boasting, emulating others who are successful, and generally trying to give an impression of superiority.

3. An easy embarrassment. This is occasioned by an inability to express definite decisions, a fear of meeting people, reticence, and lack of self-confidence. It often

results in fear of those in higher authority, avoidance of responsibility, and lack of personal initiative.

Fear of criticism is almost as general as fear of poverty. Similarly, it saps initiative and prevents the full play of the imagination, thus undermining two essential ingredients for personal achievement and success.

Fear of criticism results in not creating plans and acting because of what other people might think, do, or say. This is one of your most dangerous ghostly enemies, because it often exists in your subconscious mind and you may not even know it is there.

If You Fear Criticism

Let's examine more symptoms of the fear of criticism. The majority of people permit relatives, friends, and the public to influence them so much that they can't enjoy life because they fear being criticized.

- Countless numbers of men and women permit relatives to wreck their lives in the name of family duty because they fear criticism. Duty does not require you to submit to the destruction of your personal ambitions and the right to live your own life in your own way.
- People refuse to take chances in business because they fear the criticism that may follow if they fail.

The fear of criticism in such cases is stronger than the desire for success.

- Too many people refuse to set high goals for themselves because they fear criticizing relatives and friends who may say, "Don't aim so high, people will think you're crazy."

When Andrew Carnegie suggested I devote 20 years to the organization of a philosophy of individual achievement, my first impulse was fear of what people might say. His suggestion was far greater than anything I had ever conceived for myself. My first instinct was to create excuses, all of them traceable to the fear of criticism.

Something inside me said, "You can't do it—the job is too big and requires too much time. What will your relatives think of you? How will you earn a living? No one has ever organized a philosophy of success, what right have you to believe you can do it? Who are you, anyway, to aim so high? Remember your humble birth—what do you know about philosophy? People will think you're crazy! (And they did.) Why hasn't someone else done this before now?"

These and many other questions flashed into my mind. It seemed as if the whole world had suddenly turned its attention to me with the purpose of ridiculing me into giving up all desire to carry out Mr. Carnegie's suggestion.

Later in life, after having analyzed thousands of people, I discovered that most ideas are stillborn. To grow, ideas need the breath of life injected into them through definite plans of immediate action. The time to nurse an idea is at the time of its birth. Every minute it lives gives it a better chance of surviving. The fear of criticism is what kills most ideas that never reach the planning and action stage.

Just how humans originally came by this fear of criticism, no one can state definitely, but one thing is certain—we now have it in a highly developed form. Some believe that this fear made its appearance about the time that politics became a "profession." Others believe it can be traced to the age when women first began to concern themselves with wearing apparel styles.

> **Ideas need the breath of life injected into them through definite plans of immediate action.**

This author, being neither a humorist nor a prophet, is inclined to attribute the basic fear of criticism to the part of human inherited nature that prompts him not only to take away other people's goods and wares, but to justify the action by criticizing a person's character. It is a well known fact that a thief will criticize the person from whom he steals—that politicians seek office, not by displaying their own virtues and qualifications, but by attempting to besmirch their opponents.

Astute clothing manufacturers have not been slow to capitalize on this basic fear of criticism, with which all humankind has been cursed. Every season the styles change in many articles of wearing apparel. Who establishes the style? Certainly not the clothing purchaser, but the manufacturer. Why do the styles change so often? The answer is obvious. So they can sell more clothes.

For the same reason the manufacturers of automobiles (with a few rare and very sensible exceptions) change styles of models every season. No one wants to drive an automobile that is not of the latest style, although the older model may actually be the better car.

We have been describing how people behave under the influence of fear of criticism as applied to the small and petty things of life.

The fear of criticism robs us of our initiative, destroys our power of imagination, limits our individuality, takes away our self-reliance, and does us damage in a hundred other ways. Parents often do their children irreparable injury by criticizing them. The mother of one of my boyhood friends used to punish him with a switch almost daily, always completing the job with the statement, "You'll land in the penitentiary before you're twenty." He was sent to a reformatory at the age of seventeen.

Criticism is the one form of service, of which everyone has too much. Everyone has a stock of it that is handed out freely, whether called for or not. Our nearest relatives often are the worst offenders. It should be recognized as a crime (in reality, it is a crime of the worst nature), for any parent to build inferiority complexes in the mind of a child, through unnecessary criticism.

Employers who understand human nature, get the best out of their employees, not by criticism, but by constructive suggestion. Parents may accomplish the same results with their children.

Criticism plants fear in the human heart, or resentment—it will *not* build love or affection.

The fear of criticism robs us of our initiative, destroys our power of imagination, limits our individuality, takes away our self-reliance, and does damage in a hundred other ways.

Fear of Criticism Symptoms

This fear is almost as universal as the fear of poverty, and its effects are just as fatal to personal achievement, mainly because this fear destroys initiative and discourages the use of imagination.

In addition to the symptoms already mentioned, major symptoms of the fear are:

Self-Consciousness

Generally expressed through nervousness, timidity in conversation and in meeting strangers, awkward movement of the hands and limbs, shifting eyes.

Lack of Poise

Expressed through lack of voice control, nervousness in the presence of others, poor body posture, poor memory.

Personality

Lacking in firm decisions, personal charm, and ability to express definite opinions. The habit of side-stepping issues instead of meeting them squarely. Agreeing with others without careful examination of their opinions.

Inferiority Complex

The habit of expressing self-approval by word of mouth and by actions, as a means of covering up a feeling of inferiority. Using "big words" to impress others (often without knowing the real meaning of the words). Imitating others in dress, speech, and manners. Boasting of imaginary achievements. This sometimes gives a surface appearance of a feeling of superiority.

Extravagance

The habit of trying to "keep up with the Joneses," spending beyond your income.

Lack of Initiative

Failure to embrace opportunities for self-advancement, fear to express opinions, lack of confidence in your own ideas, giving evasive answers to questions asked by superiors, hesitancy of manner and speech, deceit in both words and deeds.

Lack of Ambition

Mental and physical laziness, lack of self-assertion, slow to reach decisions, easily influenced by others, the habit of criticizing others behind their backs and flattering them to their faces, the habit of accepting defeat without protest, quitting an undertaking when opposed by others, suspicious of other people without cause, lack of tactfulness in manner and speech, unwillingness to accept the blame for mistakes.

Self-Confidence Formula

To counteract and outwit the criticism ghost, building up your self-confidence is key. The following is a formula for you to consider speaking aloud as well as following the instructions every time you are haunted by the fear of criticism. Try reading the formula out loud at the end of each chapter to help instill the ideas within your mind:

1. I realize the dominating thoughts of my mind will eventually reproduce themselves in outward, physical action, and gradually transform themselves into physical reality; therefore, I will concentrate my thoughts for 30 minutes daily, upon the task of thinking of the person I intend to become, thereby creating in my mind a clear mental picture.

2. I know that I have the ability to achieve the object of my definite purpose in life; therefore, I demand of myself persistent, continuous action toward its attainment, and I here and now promise to render such action.

3. I know through the principle of autosuggestion, any desire that I persistently hold in my mind will eventually seek expression through some practical means of attaining the object back of it; therefore, I will

devote 10 minutes daily to demanding of myself the development of self-confidence.

4. I have clearly written down a description of my definite chief aim in life, and I will never stop trying, until I shall have developed sufficient self-confidence for its attainment.

5. I fully realize that no wealth or position can long endure, unless built upon truth and justice; therefore, I will engage in no transaction that does not benefit all whom it affects.

6. I will succeed by attracting to myself the forces I wish to use, and the cooperation of other people. I will induce others to serve me, because of my willingness to serve others.

7. I will eliminate hatred, envy, jealousy, selfishness, and cynicism, by developing love for all humanity, because I know that a negative attitude toward others can never bring me success.

8. I will cause others to believe in me, because I will believe in them, and in myself.

9. I will sign my name to this formula, commit it to memory, and repeat it aloud once a day, with full faith that it will gradually influence my thoughts and actions so that I will become a self-reliant and successful person—not believing the lies of the ghost of criticism.

– Reflection Journal –

Use the space below to capture your insights. Be honest and detailed. Writing by hand strengthens clarity and awareness.

Prompt

- How has fear of others' opinions held you back from pursuing your purpose?
- How can self-confidence be the cure-all for excommunicating the fear of criticism ghost?

My Reflections

Daily Affirmation

Speak this out loud, with conviction. Repetition builds belief, and belief transforms into action.

Affirmation for This Chapter

> ***"I trust my own judgment and act with confidence. My worth is not defined by others' opinions."***

- ❑ **Repeat** it **3 times aloud.**
- ❑ **Write** it here once, slowly and deliberately:

Action Step

Choose one small action you can take this week to apply what you've learned.

Chapter 3

ILL HEALTH

Powerful and mighty is the human mind! It builds or destroys.

This ghostly fear may be traced to both physical and social heredity. It is closely associated, as to its ghastly origin, with the causes of fear of old age and the fear of death. It leads people closely to the border of "terrible worlds" we know nothing about, but about which we have been taught some discomforting stories.

The ill health opinion is somewhat general so that certain unethical people engaged in the business of "selling health" have had not a little to do with keeping alive the fear of ill health.

In the main, we fear ill health because of the terrible pictures that have been planted in our minds of the ill health that *may* happen before death overtakes us. We also fear it because of the economic toll it may claim.

A reputable physician estimated that 75 percent of all people who visit physicians for professional service are suffering with hypochondria (imaginary illness). It has been shown most convincingly that the fear of disease, even where there is not the slightest cause for fear, often produces the physical symptoms of the disease feared.

Powerful and mighty is the human mind! It builds or destroys.

Playing upon this common weakness of fear of ill health, dispensers of patent medicines have reaped fortunes. This form of imposition upon credulous humanity became so prevalent some years ago that *Colliers' Weekly Magazine* conducted a bitter campaign against some of the worst offenders in the patent medicine business.

During the "flu" epidemic that broke out during the World War, the mayor of New York City took drastic steps to check the damage people were doing themselves through their inherent fear of ill health. He called in the newspapers and said, "Gentlemen, I feel it necessary to ask you not to publish any scare headlines concerning the 'flu' epidemic. Unless you cooperate with me, we will have a situation which we cannot control." The newspapers quit publishing stories about the "flu," and within one month the epidemic had been successfully checked.

Ill by Suggestion

Through a series of experiments conducted some years ago, it was proved that people may be made ill by suggestion. We conducted this experiment by causing three acquaintances to visit the "victims," each of whom asked the question, "What ails you? You look terribly ill." The first questioner usually provoked a grin, and a nonchalant "Oh, nothing, I'm alright," from the victim.

The second questioner usually was answered with the statement, "I don't know exactly, but I do feel badly." The third questioner was usually met with the frank admission that the victim was actually feeling ill.

Try this on an acquaintance if you doubt that it will make him uncomfortable, but do not carry the experiment too far. There is a certain religious sect whose members take vengeance upon their enemies by the "hexing" method. They call it "placing a spell" on the victim—preying on the power of suggestion.

There is overwhelming evidence that disease sometimes begins in the form of negative thoughts. Such an impulse may be passed from one mind to another, by suggestion, or created by an individual in his own mind.

Every form of negative thinking may cause ill health.

Doctors send patients into new climates for their health, because a change of "mental attitude" is necessary. The seed of fear of ill health lives in every human mind. Worry, fear, discouragement, disappointment in love and business affairs, cause this seed to germinate and grow. Business depression keeps doctors on the run, because every form of negative thinking may cause ill health.

Business and Love Disappointments

Disappointments in business and in love stand at the head of the list of causes of fear of ill health. For example, a young man suffered a disappointment in love that sent him to a hospital. For months he hovered between life and death.

A specialist in suggestive therapeutics was called in. The specialist changed nurses, placing the patient in the care of a very charming young woman who began (by pre-arrangement with the doctor) to make loving advancements toward him the first day of her arrival on the job.

Within three weeks the patient was discharged from the hospital, still suffering, but with an entirely different malady—*he was in love again.* The remedy was a hoax, but the patient and the nurse were later married. Both are in good health at the time of this writing.

Fear of Ill Health Symptoms

The symptoms of this almost universal fear:

Autosuggestion

The habit of negative use of self-suggestion by looking for, and expecting to find the symptoms of all kinds of disease. "Enjoying" imaginary illness and speaking of it as being real. The habit of trying all "fads" and "isms" recommended by others as having therapeutic value. Talking to others about operations, accidents, and other forms of illness. Experimenting with diets, physical exercises, and reducing systems without professional guidance. Trying home remedies, patent medicines, and "quack" remedies.

Hypochondria

The habit of talking of illness, concentrating the mind upon disease, and expecting its appearance until a nervous break occurs. Nothing that comes in bottles can cure this condition. It is brought on by negative thinking, and nothing but positive thought can affect a cure. Hypochondria (medical term for imaginary disease), is said to do as much damage on occasion, as the disease the person fears might do. Most so-called cases of "nerves" come from imaginary illness.

Exercise

Fear of ill health often interferes with proper physical exercise and results in becoming overweight, by causing the person to avoid outdoor life.

Susceptibility

Fear of ill health breaks down Nature's body resistance, and creates a favorable condition for any form of disease. The fear of ill health often is related to the fear of poverty, especially in the case of the hypochondriac, who constantly worries about the possibility of having to pay doctor's bills, hospital bills, etc. This type of person spends much time preparing for sickness, talking about death, saving money for cemetery lots, and burial expenses, etc.

Self-Coddling

The habit of making a bid for sympathy, using imaginary illness as the lure. (People often resort to this trick to avoid work.) The habit of feigning illness to cover plain laziness, or to serve as an alibi for lack of ambition.

Intemperance

The habit of using alcohol or narcotics to destroy pains such as headaches, neuralgia, etc., instead of eliminating the cause. The habit of reading about illness and worrying over the possibility of being stricken by it. The habit of reading patent medicine advertisements.

Social and Physical Genetics

The fear of ill health is related to another fear, which we discuss later, the fear of death. Ill health may bring someone near death, so the social and physical heredities (inheritances) of a person tend to develop this fear.

The habits of acting and thinking in accordance with the custom or social patterns of behavior by reason of membership in a particular culture, are a person's *social heredity.* The actual physical body we receive at birth, with whatever inherent weaknesses and tendencies toward disease it may have, comprise *physical heredity.*

There is overwhelming evidence that a disease can originate from a negative thought that the person continues to sell internally through autosuggestion, until the physical symptoms of that disease actually occur within the person.

Many medical doctors agree that there is a definite relationship between the patient's mental attitude and his or her physical condition. If this be so, then it follows that you can guarantee yourself sound physical health consciousness whereby you expect, demand, and receive health-sustaining elements from your food, the fresh air, and sunshine!

Creative Vision Character Traits

People with creative vision know that they can succeed only by helping others succeed, and they know also that it is not

There is a definite relationship between the patient's mental attitude and his or her physical condition.

necessary for another to fail for them to succeed. They are less likely to be affected by the ghosts of fear.

- The person with creative vision produces results instead of alibis. If they make mistakes, as we all do, they are not afraid to accept responsibility for them, and never try to shift that responsibility to another.
- Creative people make decisions quickly, but likewise make changes when they realize a wrong decision was made. They have no fear of others, either of higher or lower rank than themselves, for they are at peace with their own conscience, they are fair with others, and honest.
- The person with creative vision understands the benefits of sharing blessings, experiences, and opportunities with others, recognizing that only

by this method can he or she attain and enjoy enduring prosperity, happiness and the respect of others.

- The person with creative vision also understands that combined creative vision of several minds, directed toward a definite end in a spirit of harmony, is the very heart of the master mind principle and that this type of creative vision is a tremendous source of power.

These are some of the traits of character of which creative vision is born. These are plain words, but people of sound character and creative vision relish plain speaking.

> **Personal achievement, power, fame, and riches have a definite price, and the creative vision person is willing to pay it.**

One of the common weaknesses of most of us is that we look with envy at people who have attained noteworthy success, taking stock of them during the hour of their triumph without taking note of the price each had to pay for success. And we erroneously believe that they owe their success to some sort of pull, luck, or dishonesty.

Personal achievement, power, fame, and riches: each has a definite price, and the person with creative vision not only knows the price but is willing to pay it.

Creative Imagination

Creative imagination is something the majority of people never use during an entire lifetime. And if they do use it, it usually happens by mere accident. Only a small number of people deliberately use their creative imagination for a specific purpose. Those who voluntarily use this sense with understanding of its functions, are geniuses.

Ill health fear prevents the use of your creative imagination. Whereas a free flowing mind encourages and accepts ideas, concepts, or hunches that flash into your mind and come from one or more of the following sources:

- Your subconscious mind, which stores every thought and impression that ever reached your brain through any of the five senses.
- From another person's subconscious storehouse.
- From another person's mind who has released the thought, idea, or concept, through conscious thought.

- Infinite Intelligence.

There are no other possible sources from which "inspired" ideas or "hunches" are received.

When brain action has been stimulated, it has the effect of lifting you far above the horizon of ordinary thought. It permits you to envision distance, scope, and quality of thoughts not available on the lower plane, such as when you are solving routine problems of life or business—or feeling the fear of ill health.

Your creative imagination will never function while any of the three negatives discussed in the beginning of the book—*indecision, doubt, fear*—remain in your mind. Creative imagination is the direct link between your finite mind and Infinite Intelligence.

All revelations and discoveries take place through creative imagination.

When you are lifted to a higher level of thought through mind stimulation, it is as though you have taken off in an airplane.

You can now see over and beyond the horizon that limits your vision when you are on the ground. Not only that, but while you are on this higher level of thought, you are not even aware of problems such as gaining the three basic necessities of food, clothing, and shelter. You are in a world of thought in which the ordinary, work-a-day thoughts have been removed—just as the hills and valleys that obstruct your vision on the ground don't interfere when you are in an airplane.

While on this exalted plane of thought, the creativeness of the mind is given freedom for action—there is no room for the ill health fear ghost. The way has been cleared for the sixth sense to function. It becomes receptive to ideas that could not reach an individual under any other circumstances. The sixth sense marks the difference between a genius and an ordinary individual.

Fear is the greatest single obstacle to success.

All of us suffer from fear. What is it? Fear is an emotion intended to help preserve our lives by warning us of danger. Hence, fear can be a blessing when it raises its flag of caution so we pause and study a situation before making a decision or taking action. Too often, though, people let fear rule all their decisions and actions.

We must control fear rather than permit it to control us. Once it has served its emotional purpose as a warning signal, we must not permit it to enter into the logical reasoning on which we decide a course of action.

US President Franklin D. Roosevelt's famous words—"We have nothing to fear but fear itself"—are as applicable now, and at any time, as when he uttered them during the Great Depression.

How can you overcome your fears? First of all, by looking them full in the face—by consciously saying, "I am afraid." And then asking yourself, "Of what? What am I afraid of?"

Security

Some people's every yearning is for a sort of overall protection summed up in the catch-all cliché of "security."

The truly successful person doesn't think in these terms. The successful person's reasoning is based on creativeness and productivity. As former US President Eisenhower said, "One can attain a high degree of security in a prison cell if that's all he wants out of life."

The successful person is one who is willing to take risks, to overcome fear, when sound logic shows they are necessary to reach the desired goal.

With that one question, "What am I afraid of?" you have begun analyzing the situation facing you. You are on the road of reason that will carry you past the emotional obstacle of the fear of ill health ghost.

The next step is to consider the fear from every facet. What are the actual risks? Is the expected reward worth taking? What are other possible courses of action? What unexpected problems may be encountered? Do I have all the necessary data, statistics, and facts at hand? What have others done in similar situations, and what were the results?

Once you have completed your study, take action—immediately!

Procrastination leads only to more doubt and fear.

A noted psychologist once said that a woman, alone at night and imagining she hears noises, can settle her fears quickly. All she has to do is put one foot on the floor. In doing so, she has taken the first step on a positive course of action toward overcoming her fear.

People seeking success must force themselves in the same way to control their fears by taking the first step toward their goal.

And remember, no one walks the road of life alone. One of the most consoling—and truest—assurances given us is found in the Bible: "Fear not, I am with you always." Faith in those words will give you spiritual strength to meet any situation—physical or emotional, imagined or real.

– Reflection Journal –

Use the space below to capture your insights. Be honest and detailed. Writing by hand strengthens clarity and awareness.

Prompt

- When has worry about health affected your peace of mind more than actual illness? How can you replace fear with faith?
- How often do you pay attention to free flowing ideas, concepts, or hunches that flash into your mind? How receptive are you to eliminating ill health thoughts and replacing each with positive, healthy, even joyful thoughts?

My Reflections

Daily Affirmation

Speak this out loud, with conviction. Repetition builds belief, and belief transforms into action.

Affirmation for This Chapter

> ***"My thoughts nurture my health. I fill my mind with strength, vitality, and peace."***

- ❑ **Repeat** it **3 times aloud.**
- ❑ **Write** it here once, slowly and deliberately:

Action Step

Choose one small action you can take this week to apply what you've learned.

Chapter 4

LOVE LOSS

One of the great blessings in this world can be yours.

The fourth basic fear, the fear of the loss of love, stems from the basic need for love that every human being has, and is aggravated by the tremendous competition that goes on in the selection of a mate. It is the fear upon which jealousy is based. It is probably the most dangerous of all fears for it sometimes leads to permanent mental unbalance. It can also be very costly.

Considering the important aspects of love, there is no reason why you should harbor this fear. The affectionate response between man and woman, which is the type of love one most fears losing, is one of the great blessings in this world, and it can be yours, very surely yours, if you pursue it with a positive mental attitude and are willing to pay its price. This holds true of the other forms of love which also are so very important to the individual, as, for example, the love of parents for children and children for parents.

The love we most fear losing is one of the great blessings—and it can be very surely yours if you pursue it with a positive attitude and are willing to pay its price.

There is a law, which we may properly call the law of attraction, through the operation of which water seeks its level, and everything throughout the universe of a like nature seeks its kind. If it were not for this law, which is as immutable as the law of gravitation that keeps the planets in their proper places, the cells out of which an oak tree grows might scamper away and become mixed with the cells out of which the poplar grows, thereby producing a tree that would be part poplar and part oak. But such a phenomenon has never been heard of.

Following this law of attraction a little further, we can see how it works out among men and women. We know that successful, prosperous people seek the companionship of their own kind, while the down-and-outers seek their kind, and this happens just as naturally as water flows downhill.

Like attracts like—an indisputable fact.

Because it is true that people are constantly seeking the companionship of those whose ideas and thoughts harmonize with their own, can you see the importance of controlling and directing your thoughts and ideals so you will eventually develop exactly the kind of "magnet" in your brain to serve as an attraction in drawing others to you?

And because it is true that the very presence of any thought in your conscious mind has a tendency to arouse your body to activity that will correspond with the nature of the thought, can you see the advantage of selecting, with care, the thoughts you allow your mind to dwell on?

Traveling Out of Ghostly Territory

Read these lines carefully, think over and digest the meaning they convey, because we are now laying the foundation for a scientific truth that constitutes the very foundation on which all worthwhile human accomplishment is based. We are beginning, now, to build the roadway over which you will travel *out* of the wilderness of doubt, discouragement, uncertainty and failure—and I want you to familiarize yourself with every inch of this road.

Thought—A Powerful Form of Energy

No one knows what thought is, but every philosopher and every person of scientific ability who has given any study to the subject is in accord with the statement that thought is a powerful form of energy that directs the activities of the human body; that every idea held in the mind through prolonged, concentrated thought takes on permanent form and continues to affect body/physical activities according to its nature, either consciously or unconsciously.

Autosuggestion—which is nothing more or less than an idea held in the mind, through thought—is the only known principle through which people may literally make themselves over, after any pattern they may choose.

First, and most important of all, in my search for the rainbow's end I found God in a very concrete, unmistakable and satisfying manifestation, which is quite sufficient if I had found nothing more. All my life I had been somewhat unsettled in my own mind as to the exact nature of that Unseen Hand that directs the affairs of the universe, but my seven turning points on the rainbow trail of life brought me, at last, to a conclusion that satisfied. Whether or not my conclusion is right or wrong is not of much importance—the main thing is that it satisfied me.

Life Lessons Learned

The lessons of lesser importance which I learned are these:

> I learned that those whom we consider our enemies are, in reality, our friends. In the light of all that has happened I would not begin to go back and undo a single one of my challenging experiences, because

each one of them brought me positive evidence of the soundness of the Golden Rule (do to others as you would have them do to you) and the existence of the law of compensation through which we claim our rewards for virtue and pay the penalties for our ignorance.

I learned that Time is the friend of all who base their thoughts and actions on Truth and Justice, and that it is the mortal enemy of all who fail to do so, even though the penalty or the reward is often slow in arriving where it is due.

I learned that the only pot of gold worth striving for is that which comes from the satisfaction of knowing that our efforts are bringing happiness to others. One by one I have seen those who were unjust and who tried to destroy me, cut down by failure. I have lived to see every one of them reduced to failure far beyond anything that they planned for me. The banker was reduced to poverty; the men who stole my interest in the Betsy Ross Candy Company and tried to destroy my reputation have come down to what looks to be permanent failure, one of them being a convict in the federal prison. The man who defrauded me out of my $100,000 salary, and whom I elevated to wealth and influence, has been reduced to poverty and want. At every turn of the road which led, finally, to my rainbow's end, I saw undisputable

> evidence to back the Golden Rule philosophy that I am now sending forth, through organized effort, to hundreds of thousands of people.
>
> Last, I have learned to listen for the ringing of the bell that guides me when I come to the crossroads of doubt and hesitancy. I have learned to tap a heretofore unknown Source from which I get my promptings when I wish to know which way to turn and what to do, and these promptings have never led me in the wrong direction and I am confident they never will.

As I finish these lines I see, on the walls of my study, the pictures of great men whose laudable characters I have tried to emulate. Among them is that of the immortal Abraham Lincoln, from whose rugged, care-worn face I seem to see a smile emerging and from whose lips I can all but hear those humbling words, "With charity for all and malice toward none," and deep down in my heart I hear the mysterious bell ringing and following it comes, once more, as I close these lines, the greatest message that ever reached my consciousness: "Standeth God within the shadow of every failure."

There is no death! The stars go down
To rise upon some other shore,
And bright in heaven's jewelled crown
They shine forever more.

There is no death! The leaves may fall.
And flowers may fade and pass away;
They only wait, through wintry hours,
The warm sweet breath of May.

—John Luckey McCreery (1835–1906)

The Ultimate Love Loss

If there is a crime in all the world that causes the all-seeing God to tremble with pity and angels to weep with grief and the planets of the universe to go out of their accustomed paths, it is the crime of wholesale murder, called war!

On November 11 (1918) we are reminded of the end of the most destructive war the world had ever witnessed; a war that sent millions of human souls into eternity. Let us stop, now, and take inventory of civilization's gain from that war.

On the debit side of the ledger let us write the tragic story of pestilence and famine sweeping over Russia like a mighty tornado; and the story of intolerance and hate that has been written on the hearts of the people of every nation engaging in that war; and the famine that swept over China like a beast of prey, cutting down millions of innocent human beings. And here in our own beloved America, where the results of the inventory are more impressive because all who will look may see the effects, let us add to the indictment against this monster called war, the story of idle factories and unemployed men and disturbed relationship between employer and employee.

And, on the credit side of the inventory—what?

Absolutely nothing—nothing except unimpeachable evidence that war is a game of murder in which the winner is also the loser. As we mourn the loss of Americans who sleep beneath the sod in Flanders Felds and other faraway depths, may we never forget the sacrifice and may we instead fill the hearts of the peoples with the love of God, through organized education, so they will never again tolerate war. In the name of God, amen!

No North, no South, no East, no West,
But one great nation Heaven blest.
No Jew or Gentile, no race or creed,
Just more love of God is all we poor mortals need.

—Napoleon Hill

Recognize that love and affection constitute the finest medicines for both your body and your soul. Love changes the entire chemistry of the body and conditions it for the expression of a positive mental attitude. And love also extends the space you may occupy in the hearts of others. And in this connection, it is important to remember that *while love is free, the best way to receive it is to give it.*

Keep a daily diary of your good deeds on behalf of others, and never let the sun set on a single day without recording some act of human kindness. The benefits of this habit will be cumulative, and eventually it will give you domain over great spaces in the hearts of others. And remember—one good deed each day keeps old man gloom away.

Love and affection are the finest medicines for both your body and your soul.

For every favor or benefit you receive, give an equal benefit to others. The law of increasing returns will operate in your favor and eventually, perhaps very soon, it will give you the capacity to get everything you are entitled to receive. A positive mental attitude must have a two-way highway on which to travel, or it will cease to function.

Fear of Love Loss Symptoms

The distinguishing symptoms of this fear:

A positive mental attitude must travel on a two-way highway, or it will cease to function.

Jealousy

The habit of being suspicious of friends and loved ones without any reasonable evidence of sufficient grounds. (Jealousy is a form of schizophrenia, sometimes becomes violent without the slightest cause.) The habit of accusing wife or husband of infidelity without grounds. General suspicion of everyone, absolute faith in no one.

Fault Finding

The habit of finding fault with friends, relatives, business associates, and loved ones upon the slightest provocation, or without any cause whatsoever.

Gambling

The habit of gambling, stealing, cheating, and otherwise taking hazardous chances to provide money for loved ones, with the belief that love can be bought. The habit of spending beyond the person's means, or incurring debts, to provide gifts for loved ones, with the object of making a favorable showing. Insomnia, nervousness, lack of persistence, weakness of will, lack of self-control, lack of self-reliance, bad temper.

– Reflection Journal –

Use the space below to capture your insights. Be honest and detailed. Writing by hand strengthens clarity and awareness.

Prompt

- How have jealousy or insecurity affected your relationships? What would trust and generosity look like instead?
- How could your life be improved if you were to use the powerful energy of concentrated thought to focus on your goals?

My Reflections

Daily Affirmation

Speak this out loud, with conviction. Repetition builds belief, and belief transforms into action.

Affirmation for This Chapter

> ***"I give and receive love freely. My relationships are grounded in trust, gratitude, and faith."***

- ❑ **Repeat** it **3 times aloud.**
- ❑ **Write** it here once, slowly and deliberately:

____

____

____

____

____

____

____

____

____

____

Action Step

Choose one small action you can take this week to apply what you've learned.

Chapter 5

FEAR OF OLD AGE

When you sell yourself on the idea of youth rather than old age, you will attract a more youthful look and feel.

In the main, the fear of old age ghost grows out of two sources. First, the thought that old age may bring with it poverty. Second, the possibility of ill health, which is more common as people grow older, is also a contributing cause of this common fear of old age.

In the basic fear of old age, there are two very sound reasons for apprehension—one growing out of a distrust of others who may seize whatever worldly goods we may possess, and the other arising from terrible stories of the "world beyond," perhaps planted in our minds through social heredity before we came into full possession of our mind.

Eroticism also enters into the cause of the fear of old age, as no one cherishes the thought of diminishing sexual attraction.

But the most common cause of old age fear is associated with the possibility of poverty. "Poorhouse" is not a pretty word, and not one even used much these days. It throws a chill into the mind of every person who faces the possibility of having to spend their declining years on a "poor farm," nursing home, and the like.

Another contributing cause of the fear of old age, is the possibility of loss of freedom and independence, as old age may bring with it the loss of both physical and economic freedom.

Fear of old age is the fifth basic fear. I like to jump on this fear with both feet and to laugh about it—because it is a lot better to laugh than to cry. When you have a birthday, take a year *off* your age instead of adding one. Thus you will begin to feel younger and to change in appearance so that you will actually look younger. When you sell yourself on the idea of youth rather than old age, you will attract a more youthful look and feel.

Nature compensates you for the loss of youth with one of the greatest gifts—wisdom.

It has been discovered that some of the men of greatest achievement have done their life's best work after 55, and some even after 60 and 70. The reason for this is that nature compensates you for the loss of youth with one of the greatest things in the world—wisdom. Wisdom comes from experience, and experience comes with age.

We have good times when we are 20, 25, and 30, but when we have passed these years, we would not choose to go back to them again. *We are more useful to the world as we mature.* True enough, we can no longer stay up such long hours and get around as well at night, but most of these activities disappear with maturity.

Faith Versus Fear

Outwitting the fear of old age can be done so with follow-through faith, or applied faith—the dynamo of this science of personal achievement philosophy because it enables action. Faith is the state of mind where you relax your own reason and willpower to open yourself completely to the inflow of power from Infinite Intelligence.

When you apply faith, you accept guidance from Infinite Intelligence. Turning over problems to this guidance can be difficult, until you realize that if you let it, the creative force of the entire universe can aid you in all your endeavors.

Faith is a mental attitude wherein the mind is cleared of all fears and doubts and directed toward attaining something definite through the aid of Infinite Intelligence. With faith we can tap into and draw on the power of Infinite Intelligence at will. Faith is guidance from within, but nothing more. It will not bring you what you desire, but it will show you the path to travel to go after whatever you desire.

Faith acts through the brain cells of the subconscious mind, the subconscious acting as the gateway between the conscious mind and Infinite Intelligence. Keep that gateway open. Keep it free from self-imposed limitations—for Infinite Intelligence recognizes no such reality as limitations, except those imposed by an individual and those that call for a circumvention or a suspension of natural laws.

To apply your faith to success, you need to clear all doubts and fears from your mind, then direct your mind toward the attainment of something definite. If you allow it, help will follow.

Every person has the power to condition their mind for the expression of faith. Every person has this power, because every person has been provided by the Creator with complete control over his or her own mind. In fact, this is the only thing over which any person has complete control.

The vast majority of people keep their minds trained on all the things they fear and do *not* want, including the fear of poverty, ill health, criticism, the loss of love and affection, and old age. And when you train your mind on fears, they always have a strange way of materializing.

People who have found the way to successful achievement keep their minds trained on the things they *do* want. And by their thinking, they condition their minds for the expression of that mysterious power known as faith. These people don't dwell on their age, they focus on what good they can do today, and tomorrow, and....

Faith has been called the mainspring of the soul, through which our aims, desires, plans, and purposes may become reality. It is an indefinite business you can build with the power of faith.

Fear of Old Age Symptoms

The most common symptoms of this fear:

- The tendency to slow down and develop an inferiority complex at the age of mental maturity, around the age of 40, falsely believing that they are "slipping" because of age. (The truth is that people's most useful years, mentally and spiritually, are between 40 and beyond!)
- The habit of speaking apologetically of themselves as "being old" merely because they reached a certain age—instead of reversing the rule and expressing gratitude for having reached the age of wisdom and understanding.
- The habit of killing off initiative, imagination, and self-reliance by falsely believing they are too old to exercise these qualities. (There is nothing wrong with the man or woman of 50 dressing with

the aim of trying to appear younger and affecting mannerisms of youth, thus keeping a youthful state of mind.)

No matter the age, personal initiative heads the list of qualities a successful and vital person needs to incorporate into life to remain productive:

- Personal initiative.
- Adoption a definite major purpose.
- Motivation to inspire continuous action in pursuit of a definite major purpose.
- A master mind alliance through which you may acquire the power to attain your definite purpose.
- Self-reliance in proportion to the scope and object of your major purpose.
- Self-discipline sufficient to insure mastery of the head and the heart, and to sustain your motives until they have been realized.
- Persistence, based on the will to win.
- A well-developed imagination, controlled and directed.
- The habit of reaching definite and prompt decisions.
- The habit of basing opinions on known facts instead of relying on guesswork.
- The habit of going the extra mile.

- The capacity to generate enthusiasm at will, and to control it.
- A well-developed sense of details.
- The capacity to take criticism without resentment.
- Familiarity with the ten basic motives that inspire all human action.
- The capacity to concentrate your full attention upon one task at a time.
- Willingness to accept full responsibility for the mistakes of subordinates.
- The habit of recognizing the merits and abilities of others.
- A positive mental attitude at all times.
- The habit of assuming full responsibility for any job or task undertaken.
- The capacity for applied faith.
- Patience with subordinates and associates.
- The habit of following through with any task once begun.
- The habit of emphasizing thoroughness instead of speed.
- Dependability, the only requirement of leadership that can be stated with one word—but no less important to success on that account.

These qualities are important in any endeavor you may be interested in. Concentrating on these traits consciously or unconsciously will eliminate the fear of old age.

The most intense yearning of every normal person is for recognition of his or her value and worth as an individual human being.

More than money, more than fame, more than any material thing, this is the greatest reward you can give anyone—to let people know that you appreciate them for themselves alone, rather than for what they can do for you. Feigning old age is the opposite of exuding a youthful, vital existence that will make your home, neighborhood, community, and beyond a better place.

Recognition and Appreciation

Humanity's fate is, in essence, a lonely one, and may be exacerbated by the passing of years. Except for faith in the Creator, each is born alone and dies alone. Although it may be possible to postpone someone's death through our own sacrifice, no one actually can die for another.

Each ultimately faces the end of earthly existence as a matter strictly between the person and God. It is this subconscious realization that causes us our essential loneliness, that causes us to strive so mightily for the appreciation of others.

Psychiatrists and psychologists are coming to realize, as philosophers and priests have realized for centuries, that this is the basic drive of humankind—not sex or the urge for security, but the demand for simple, egotistical recognition.

None of us has so long to live that we can afford to waste a precious moment in such a negative way as carping criticisms of others. But every moment spent in praise of someone else rebounds to our own credit—no matter our age. For nowhere is it more true that like begets like than in this instance.

That doesn't mean that you must engage in fatuous flattery or apple polishing. Nor does it mean you must overlook errors and ineptness in subordinates.

But it does mean that every word of criticism you offer should be given in a spirit of helpful instructiveness, with a view to making the subject a better person, a better worker, a better family member than before. It also means that you are willing to recognize the good points as well as the bad and give them greater weight of appreciation.

It will help you, too, to remember than no man or woman is entirely free of the drive for recognition. That includes your superiors, subordinates, spouse, and strangers. Your boss at this moment is probably more tired, more lonely, and more disheartened than you realize. He or she would appreciate a word of sincere praise from you every bit as much as the one you hope to receive.

As a matter of tactfulness, too, beware of the person who invites you to "Go ahead and criticize me. I want your honest opinion." Few of us are so self-disciplined that we actually enjoy criticism. Such an invitation is merely a sign of a person's need for recognition—no matter the age.

Humankind's greatest punishment for miscreants lies not in the bars and strict discipline of prison life. It's in the eradication of the prisoner's individuality—the uniforms, the numbers, the deliberate withdrawal of recognition.

The true leader in the military service carefully guards the individual ego of each subordinate. Although realizing the need for discipline and uniformity, a leader also realizes the inherent dangers they hold as killers of personality and spirit. Hence, the true friend, the true leader makes sure that every person knows they are valued and respected as an individual.

Vital and Vibrant

By adopting the same attitude, you will be taking a tremendous step toward rejecting the fear of old age by becoming a vibrant person yourself.

Form the habit of tolerance and keep an open mind on all subjects, toward people of all races and creeds and ages. Learn to like people just as they are, instead of demanding of them that they be as you wish them to be.

Avoid the fear of old age by remembering that the Creator so blessed humankind that nothing is ever taken from us without something of equal or greater value given in return. Through the operation of this profound plan, youth is replaced by wisdom.

It may help you to accept and appreciate this truth if you are reminded that the greatest achievements usually take place after we are well beyond the age of 50.

Let your motto be: Deeds, not mere words.

Fears and Curses

The prevalence of these fears, as a curse to the world, runs in cycles. For almost six years during the Great Depression (1929–1941), Americans floundered in the cycle of entertaining the fear of poverty. During World War II (1939–1945), we were in the cycle of the fear of death. Just following the war, we were in the cycle of entertaining the fear of ill health ghost, evidenced by the epidemic of disease that spread itself worldwide.

Fears are nothing more than our state of mind—and our state of mind is subject to our control and direction. Physicians are less subject to being attacked by disease than ordinary people, because *physicians do not fear disease.* Physicians, without fear or hesitation, have been known to physically contact hundreds of people, daily, who were suffering from such contagious diseases including smallpox, without becoming infected. Their immunity against the disease consisted, largely, if not solely, in their absolute lack of *fear.*

We can create nothing that we do not first conceive in the form of an impulse of thought. Following the statement, comes another of still greater importance, namely, *our thought impulses begin immediately to translate into their physical equivalent,*

Fears are nothing more than our state of mind—and our state of mind is subject to our control and direction.

whether those thoughts are voluntary or involuntary. Thought impulses that are picked up through the ether, by mere chance (thoughts released by other minds) may determine our financial, business, professional, or social destiny—just as surely as do the thought impulses we create by intent and design.

Immunity against disease may consist in absolute lack of fear.

– Reflection Journal –

Use the space below to capture your insights. Be honest and detailed. Writing by hand strengthens clarity and awareness.

Prompt

- Do you focus more on what age takes away or what wisdom gives you? How might shifting your focus change your outlook?

- If you want to outwit the fear of old age, what steps will you take today to bust that ghost right out of your life?

My Reflections

Daily Affirmation

Speak this out loud, with conviction. Repetition builds belief, and belief transforms into action.

Affirmation for This Chapter

> ***"With every passing year, I grow wiser and more capable of fulfilling my purpose."***

- ❑ **Repeat** it **3 times aloud.**
- ❑ **Write** it here once, slowly and deliberately:

___

___

___

___

___

___

___

___

___

___

___

___

Action Step

Choose one small action you can take this week to apply what you've learned.

Chapter 6

DEATH

A desire for perpetual life is closely allied with the desire for self-preservation—instinctive in the nature of humanity.

The desire to know if there is life after death is a very strong motive to have a fear of death—and it is the one upon which nearly all religious activity is based.

Surveys have been made of the peoples of the world that show that every culture, from the lowest degree of social development to the highest, worships something. They all have some form of religion. And, oddly enough, the central theme of all such religions is immortality, or everlasting life.

Some students of this subject have suggested that perhaps the greatest evidence favoring a belief in the continuation of consciousness after earth life, lies in the persistence with which this idea recurs in all cultures. A desire for perpetual life is closely allied with the desire for self-preservation, and it is instinctive in the nature of humanity.

A desire for perpetual life is closely allied with the desire for self-preservation, and it is instinctive in the nature of humanity.

To some, this is the cruelest of all the basic fears. The reason is obvious. The terrible pangs of fear associated with the thought of death, in the majority of cases worldwide, may be charged directly to religious fanaticism. For thousands of years humankind has been asking the still unanswered questions: "Where did I come from, and where am I going?"

During my research, I reviewed a book entitled *A Catalogue of the Gods,* in which were listed the 30,000 gods man has worshiped. Think of it! Thirty thousand of them, represented by everything from a crawfish to a man. It is little wonder that people have become frightened at the approach of death.

During the darker ages of the past, the cunning and crafty were not slow to offer the answer to these after-death questions, for a price. Eternity is a long time. Fire is a terrible thing. The thought of eternal punishment, with fire, not only causes people to fear death, it often causes them to lose their reason. It can destroy interest in life and make happiness impossible.

While the religious leader may not be able to provide safe conduct into Heaven, nor by lack of such provision allow the unfortunate to descend into hell, the possibility of the latter seems so terrible that the very thought of it lays hold of the imagination in such a realistic way that it paralyzes reason, and sets up the fear of death.

Respond with one simple question when someone tries to scare you by telling you what will happen to you after death. Ask that person one simple question and stand by firmly for a reply: "How do you know?"

In truth, no person knows, and no one has ever known, what Heaven or hell is like, nor does any one know if either place actually exists. This very lack of positive knowledge opens the door of the human mind to the charlatan to enter and control that mind with a stock of various brands of pious fraud and trickery.

Insane asylums, mental hospitals, are filled with men and women who have gone mad because of the fear of death, among many other reasons. This fear is useless. Death will come, no matter what anyone may think about it. Accept it as a necessity, and pass the thought out of your mind. It must be a necessity, or it would not come to all. Perhaps it is not as bad as it has been pictured by some.

The entire world is made up of only two things, energy and matter. In elementary physics we learn that neither matter nor energy—the only two realities known—can be created nor destroyed. Both matter and energy can be transformed, but neither can be destroyed.

Life is energy, if it is anything. If neither energy nor matter can be destroyed, of course life cannot be destroyed. Life, like other forms of energy, may be passed through various processes of transition or change, but it cannot be destroyed. Death is mere transition.

If death is not mere change, or transition, then I believe that nothing comes after death except a long, eternal, peaceful sleep, and sleep is nothing to be feared. Thus you may wipe out, forever, the fear of death from your thoughts.

I finally said to myself: "Death is probably one of two things: either death is just one long eternal sleep"—and I don't know of very many things in this world I enjoy more than sleep—"or else, if it isn't sleep, it's an experience on some plane far better than we have on this earth and, in either event, there is nothing to fear because it's going to come anyway."

When you get around to reasoning like that, you take this fear of death and write it off. You don't discuss it or think about it. I can truthfully tell you I am not any more concerned with death than I am with what I am going to have for breakfast tomorrow morning. I will "go" at one time or another and there is nothing I can do about it; therefore, I would be a simple-minded person if I devoted any of my time to worrying about it.

Wonders of the Human Machine

Suppose some great person were to hand you an exquisite, beautifully built machine equipped with many self-repairing features. Suppose he explained to you that with reasonable care and proper handling, this machine would automatically, after about 18 years of warming up, begin to deliver money from a slot, each week, in gradually increasing amounts for the next 40 to 60 years. That the total amount delivered by this machine would not be less than $200,000. He might go on to say that if you really learned how to run and care for the machine like an expert, you might increase its output by millions of dollars.

Suppose the builder of this machine let you in on a little secret. He told you that there was another slot which every moment of its life produced either happiness and satisfaction, or despair and dejection. If you would learn to manipulate the controls for this slot with the deftness of an expert, the machine would purr at great speed, producing endless satisfaction and financial reward. He might warn you that it would take much patient learning and long trial and the careful following of instructions to achieve this result.

His parting words might be, "Others have done it before you, and there may be many who follow you. They all had one secret in common—they had faith in the machine and faith in me and faith in my instructions." With that, he might leave you to your own devices.

Now suppose that after many years of trial you had only half-mastered the technique, and you learned that there were other experts who could help you. True, they had mastered only small segments of the knowledge of the master who built the machine; but if each in his field could help straighten you out and thus improve the way you handle your controls and the results you achieve, would you seek their advice?

Undoubtedly you would.

Fear of Death Symptoms

The general symptom of this fear is the *habit of thinking about dying* instead of making the most of life, due generally to lack of purpose, or lack of a suitable occupation. This fear is more prevalent among the aged, but sometimes the more youthful are victims of it as well.

The greatest of all remedies for the fear of death is a burning desire for achievement, backed by useful service to others. A busy person seldom has time to think about dying. He finds life too thrilling to worry about death.

Sometimes the fear of death is closely associated with the fear of poverty, where the person's death would leave loved ones poverty-stricken. In other cases, the fear of death is caused by illness and the consequent breaking down of physical body resistance. The most common causes of the fear of death: ill health, poverty, lack of appropriate occupation, disappointment over love, insanity, religious fanaticism.

The fear of death, the seventh and last basic fear, is the grandfather of them all. This one is always difficult to whip because of the complex background of the social inheritance of many people. This is really a very strong fear—and a universal one.

Wishing and Believing

From the beginning of time, there is a tendency to fear anything we do not understand or do not have complete, absolute answers. How can we overcome this fear?

"Wishing won't make it so," runs an old saying. This is true, and helps you remember that a wish is not a belief.

A wish takes place upon the surface of the mind. "I wish...," you may say, and follow with any wish that tickles your fancy—"to have a million dollars drop into my lap...to be able to flap my arms and fly." A wish is not limited by natural forces. That very apparent fact, however, is not the main difference between a wish and a belief.

Belief in a cause—much stronger than a wish to stay alive—causes people to transcend the instinct of self-preservation.

A belief is created, as it were, in the depths of the mind. A belief becomes part of you. That is why a true, deep belief can change your glandular secretions and the content of your bloodstream, and work other physical changes beyond the power of medical science to explain.

Again, a belief, radiating its unknown wavelength from the depths of your mind to the depths of another mind, accounts for a good deal of "personality power" and much else on which we can put only the clumsiest of labels.

It is belief in a cause—much stronger than a wish to stay alive—which causes people to transcend the instinct of self-preservation. It is belief that founds religion, sustains nations, stands behind anything great that ever is achieved.

You can achieve what you believe.

A belief, I repeat, is part of you; that is why you can achieve what you believe. Moreover, when you hold a great belief that you believe all the time it will sustain you as you go on living.

If you accept defeat as an inspiration to try again, with renewed confidence and determination, the attainment of your success will be only a matter of time. If you accept defeat as final and allow it to destroy your confidence, you may as well abandon your hope of success.

Every defeat you meet will mark an important turning point in your life, for defeat will bring you face-to-face with the necessity of renewing confidence in yourself, or of admitting that confidence is lacking.

Defeat often serves to relieve a person of conceit. But there is a difference between conceit and self-reliance based on an honest inventory of your character. People who quit when defeat overtakes them indicates that they mistook their conceit for self-reliance.

If people have genuine self-reliance, they also have sound character, for one springs from the other. And a sound character does not yield to defeat without a fight.

Likewise, genuine faith in yourself to live a long and productive life, for as long as that may be, will cause that dastardly ghost of the fear of death to wither and fade away, far away.

The Law of Success

The Law of Success is a set of principles that, if followed, will fill your mind with positive, constructive thoughts—shoving aside the fear of thoughts of death. Consider carefully:

1. Set your head and heart upon a *definite major purpose* and go to work, right where you stand, to attain it; and begin *now.*

2. Adopt and follow the habit of *going the extra mile* by rendering more service and better service than you are paid for, thus enlarging the space you may occupy in the world.

3. Control your *mental attitude* and keep it always positive and free from the spirit of defeatism.

4. Apply the *Golden Rule* in all your human relationships, no matter what others may do.

5. Learn all that others have discovered in connection with your occupation, job, or business, and profit by their experience, thus saving yourself both grief and loss of time.

6. Eat sparingly, of the right combination of foods, and make sure that your "system" is always free from toxic poisoning.

7. Keep your dominating thoughts *on* what you desire and demand of life, and *off* what you do not desire.

8. Learn to transmute your sex emotion into the attainment of your definite major purpose, at will, remembering that this is a creative force of unknown, unlimited possibilities.

9. If you work for another person, do your work the boss's way, not your way, and do it in a gracious, pleasing manner.

10. Instead of criticizing others (no matter how much they may deserve it) devote your time to the discovery of traits of your own that should be corrected lest they provide the basis of just criticism against you.

If followed, in a spirit of sincerity, these ten rules will help you to occupy all the space in the world that your talents, education, and experience entitle you to enjoy—and will bring you the peace of mind that surpasses understanding.

Every defeat you meet will mark an important turning point in your life.

– Reflection Journal –

Use the space below to capture your insights. Be honest and detailed. Writing by hand strengthens clarity and awareness.

Prompt

- What beliefs shape your perspective on death? How could reframing those beliefs help you live more fully?

My Reflections

Daily Affirmation

Speak this out loud, with conviction. Repetition builds belief, and belief transforms into action.

Affirmation for This Chapter

> ***"I release the fear of death. Each day I live with faith, courage, and gratitude."***

- ❑ **Repeat** it **3 times aloud.**
- ❑ **Write** it here once, slowly and deliberately:

Action Step

Choose one small action you can take this week to apply what you've learned.

Chapter 7

DEFEATING WORRY

Worry is a form of sustained fear caused by indecision—it is a state of mind that *can* be controlled.

Worry is a state of mind based on fear. It works slowly, but persistently. It is insidious and subtle. Step by step it "digs itself in" until it paralyzes a person's reasoning and destroys self-confidence and initiative. Worry is a form of sustained fear caused by indecision; therefore, it is a state of mind that *can* be controlled.

An unsettled mind is helpless. Indecision makes an unsettled mind. Most individuals lack the willpower to reach decisions promptly, and to stand by them after they have been made, even during normal business conditions. During periods of economic unrest, individuals are handicapped, not alone by an inherent nature to be slow at reaching decisions, but is influenced by the indecision of others around who have created a state of "mass indecision."

During the Great Depression, the atmosphere worldwide was filled with "Fearenza" and "Worryitis," the two mental disease germs that began to spread themselves after the Wall Street frenzy in 1929. There is only one known antidote for these germs, and that is the habit of prompt and *firm decision.* Moreover, it is an antidote that every individual must apply for themselves.

We do not worry over conditions after we have reached a decision to follow a definite line of action. Therefore, it is critical to make decisions promptly and wisely.

I once interviewed a man who was to be electrocuted two hours later. The condemned man was the calmest of some eight men who were in the death cell with him. His calmness prompted me to ask him how it felt to know that he was going into eternity in a short while. With a smile of confidence on his face, he said, "It feels fine. Just think, brother, my troubles will soon be over. I have had nothing but trouble all my life. It has been a hardship to get food and clothing. Soon I will not need these things. I have felt fine ever since I learned for certain that I must die. I made up my mind then, to accept my fate in good spirit."

As he spoke, he devoured a dinner of proportions sufficient for three men, eating every mouthful of the food brought to him, and apparently enjoying it as much as if no disaster awaited him. A *decision* gave this man resignation to his fate! Making a decision, a choice, can also prevent our acceptance of undesired circumstances.

The six basic fears become translated into a state of worry, through indecision. And you can defeat and eradicate the ghosts of fear when you:

- Relieve yourself forever of the *fear of death,* by *choosing to accept death* as an inescapable event.
- Whip the *fear of poverty* by *choosing to get along with whatever wealth you can accumulate without worry.*
- Put your foot upon the neck of the *fear of criticism* by *choosing not to worry* about what other people think, do, or say.
- Eliminate the *fear of old age* by *choosing to accept it,* not as a handicap, but as a great blessing that carries with it wisdom, self-control, and understanding not known to youth.
- Acquit yourself of the *fear of ill health* by *choosing to forget the symptoms.*
- Master the *fear of loss of love* by *choosing to get along without love,* if that is necessary.
- Kill the habit of *worry,* in all its forms, by reaching a general, blanket decision that *nothing life has to offer is worth the price of worry.* With this decision will come poise, peace of mind, and calmness of thought that brings happiness.

People whose minds are filled with fear not only destroys their chances of intelligent action, but they transmit those destructive vibrations to the minds of all those with whom they come into contact, which also destroys their chances.

Even a dog or a horse knows when its master lacks courage; moreover, a dog or a horse will pick up the vibrations of fear thrown off by its master and behave accordingly.

Lower down the line of intelligence in the animal kingdom, there is this same capacity to pick up the vibrations of fear. A honeybee immediately senses fear in the mind of a person—and for reasons unknown, a bee will sting the person whose mind is releasing vibrations of fear, much more readily than it will molest the person whose mind registers no fear.

The vibrations of fear pass from one mind to another just as quickly and as surely as the sound of the human voice passes from the broadcasting station to the receiving set of a radio—and by the self-same medium.

I believe that mental telepathy is a reality. Thoughts pass from one mind to another, voluntarily, whether or not this fact is recognized by either the person releasing the thoughts, or the persons who pick up those thoughts.

Kickback Damage

The person who gives expression, by word of mouth, to negative or destructive thoughts is practically certain to experience the results of those words in the form of a destructive "kickback." The release of destructive thought impulses, alone, without the aid of words, produces also a "kickback" in more ways than one.

> First of all, and perhaps most important to be remembered, the person who releases thoughts of a destructive nature, must suffer damage through the breaking down of the faculty of creative imagination.
>
> Second, the presence in the mind of any destructive emotion develops a negative personality that repels people, and often converts them into antagonists.
>
> The third source of damage to the person who entertains or releases negative thoughts lies in this significant fact—these thought impulses are not only damaging to others, but they imbed themselves in the subconscious mind of the person releasing them, and there become part of his or her character.

We are never through with a thought, merely by releasing it. When a thought is released, it spreads in every direction, through the medium of the ether, but it also plants itself permanently in the subconscious mind of the person releasing it.

Your business in life is presumably to achieve success. To be successful, you must find peace of mind, acquire the material needs of life, and above all, attain happiness. All of these evidences of success begin in the form of thought impulses.

You may control your own mind, you have the power to feed it whatever thought impulses you choose. With this privilege goes also the responsibility of using it constructively. You are the master of your own earthly destiny just as surely as you have the power to control your own thoughts. You may influence, direct, and eventually control your own environment, making your life what you want it to be.

You are the master of your own earthly destiny—just as surely as you have the power to control your own thoughts.

Or, you may neglect to exercise the privilege that is yours to make your life to order, thus casting yourself upon the broad "sea of circumstance" where you will be tossed hither and yon, like a chip on the waves of the ocean.

Success Is...

Success is the most enchanting word in the English language.

Tell the average person that success is the attainment of whatever one wants in life without interfering with the rights of anyone else and that the very first step to be taken in procuring it is development of the habit of rendering more service than paid for—and your words will fall on ears that hear but do not understand.

But, tell a person that success means money, and unless that person is one of the proverbial few who really understand how to succeed, he or she will immediately show interest in your words by saying, "SURE! How can I get some of it without giving much in return?"

One of the very first jobs I ever had was that of handy-boy around a sawmill. It gave me a chance to see that a big puffing steam engine turned the machinery; that the steam in the big boiler kept the engine running; that the fireman kept the steam pouring into the engine by constantly pushing wood into the firebox.

I noticed that when the fire began to die down, the steam began to die down also; that a hot fire produced plenty of steam. Then and there I got my first lesson, in an elementary sort of way, of the principle of cause and effect.

Later in life, long after I had worked myself into a higher place than that of handy-boy around a sawmill, I saw evidence on every hand that there was a cause for everything; nothing just happened by mere accident. I saw that achievement in any undertaking depended very largely upon the amount of intelligent effort put into it; that those who achieved most were those who served best.

Worry Versus a Positive Mental Attitude

The fear of the loss of liberty, is the opposite of the desire for freedom of body and mind, one of the basic motives. And this fear is prevalent throughout the world today, for we know that certain influences are constantly and deliberately working to destroy the hard-won liberties so dear to humankind.

People all around the world, in centuries past and in more recent years, have shed precious blood to gain and maintain the personal and political liberties that we now enjoy. They are not to be taken for granted or held lightly. A positive mental attitude demands that we make the most constructive use of our liberties and be ever vigilant in their defense.

Liberty is something clearly bought and preserved only by constant vigilance.

We do not have to be prophets or possess any special perception to discern the serious threats to our liberty that are daily gaining ground in the world. One of the basic ideas of my Science of Success philosophy is that the American way of life, the democratic way of life, is essential to individual achievement on every level. Here is something worthy of your most serious thinking: We must be on the alert to preserve our liberties. Liberty is something clearly bought and preserved only by constant vigilance.

Drifters make no attempt to discipline or control their thoughts and never learn the difference between positive thinking and negative thinking. Drifters in life allow their minds to drift with any stray thought that may float into it. People who drift in connection with their thought habits are sure to drift on other subjects as well.

In my book, *Outwitting the Devil*, it was stated that the devil said he feared nothing except that the world might sometime produce a thinker who would use his own mind, adding significantly that he controlled all drifters who neglected to use their own minds. The devil is not the only one who exploits the drifter. *And drifters are the victims not only of all those who wish to exploit them, but they are also the victims of all the stray, negative thoughts that park themselves in their minds.*

Non-drifters take full possession of their own minds through self-discipline and organize definite plans and purposes. They direct their minds to whatever ends they desire keep their minds occupied with what they want and off the things they do not want.

A positive mental attitude is the first and the most important of the twelve riches of life, and that attitude cannot be attained by the drifter. It can be attained only by a scrupulous regard for time, through habits of self-discipline.

No amount of time devoted to our occupation can compensate for the benefits of a positive mental attitude, for this is the power that makes the use of time effective and productive.

A positive mental attitude does not grow voluntarily, like the weeds of the fields. It requires cultivation, through carefully disciplined habits of thoughts. And the greatest of all training grounds for the cultivation of a positive mental attitude is provided by our chosen occupation, where we spend the greatest part of our lives. Here you may combine your efforts to make them financially productive and to develop a positive mental attitude.

A positive mental attitude is the first and the most important of the twelve riches of life.

When you get your own thought habits under control, you will have yourself under control, but you cannot do it by drifting.

Organize your thoughts. Decide what you want, to what position in life you aspire. Then plan ways and means to express your thoughts, in terms of organized action. Follow through with applied faith and unremitting persistence. This is the means by which you can become the master of your fate, the captain of your soul.

Waste no time worrying about what others may think. What YOU think and do is most important.

– Reflection Journal –

Use the space below to capture your insights. Be honest and detailed. Writing by hand strengthens clarity and awareness.

Prompt

- What worries dominate your thoughts most often? How do they affect your decisions and peace of mind?
- What does becoming "the master of your fate and the captain of your soul" mean to you?

My Reflections

Daily Affirmation

Speak this out loud, with conviction. Repetition builds belief, and belief transforms into action.

Affirmation for This Chapter

> ***"I release worry and choose faith. I focus on what I can control, and I trust the rest will unfold for my good."***

- ❑ **Repeat** it **3 times aloud.**
- ❑ **Write** it here once, slowly and deliberately:

Action Step

Choose one small action you can take this week to apply what you've learned.

Chapter 8

AVOID NEGATIVE INFLUENCES

You must deal with your own faults as you would with any enemy.

In addition to the six basic fears, there is another evil by which people suffer. It constitutes a rich soil in which the seeds of failure grow abundantly. Similar to many of the other ghosts, it is so subtle that its presence often is not detected. This affliction cannot properly be classed as a fear, it is more deeply seated and more often fatal than all of the six fears. For want of a better name, let us call this *evil "susceptibility to negative influences."*

Wise people who accumulate great riches always protect themselves against this evil! The poverty stricken never do! Those who succeed in any calling must prepare their minds to resist evil. If you are reading this philosophy about fears for the purpose of accumulating riches, you should examine yourself very carefully to determine whether you are susceptible to negative influences. If you neglect this self-analysis, you will forfeit your right to attain the object of your desires.

Make your analysis thorough. After you read the questions in this chapter prepared for this self-analysis, hold yourself to a strict accounting in your answers. Go at the task as carefully as you would search for any other enemy you knew to be awaiting you in ambush and deal with your own faults as you would with a more tangible enemy.

You can easily protect yourself against highway robbers, because the law provides organized cooperation for your benefit; but the "seventh basic evil" is more difficult to master, because it strikes when you are not aware of its presence—when you are asleep and while you are awake.

Moreover, its weapon is intangible, because it consists of merely—a state of mind. This evil is also dangerous because it strikes in as many different forms as there are human experiences. Sometimes it enters the mind through the well-meant words of a person's own relatives. At other times, it bores from within, through our own mental attitude. Always it is as deadly as poison, even though it may not kill as quickly.

How to Protect Yourself from Negative Influences

To protect yourself against negative influences, whether of your own making, or the result of the activities of negative people around you:

- Recognize that you have willpower, and put it into constant use, until it builds a wall of immunity against negative influences in your own mind.
- Recognize the fact that you, and every other human being, is by nature, lazy, indifferent, and susceptible to all suggestions that harmonize with your weaknesses.
- Recognize that you are, by nature, susceptible to all six basic fears, and set up habits to counteract all these fears.
- Recognize that negative influences often work on you through your subconscious mind; therefore, they are difficult to detect.
- Keep your mind closed against all people who depress or discourage you in any way.
- Clean out your medicine chest—throw away pill bottles and stop pandering to colds, aches, pains, and imaginary illness.
- Deliberately seek the company of people who influence you to think and act for yourself.
- Do not accept troubles.

Without doubt, the most common weakness of all human beings is the habit of leaving their minds open to the negative influence of other people. This weakness is all the more damaging because most people do not recognize that they are cursed by it, and many who acknowledge it, neglect or refuse to correct the evil until it becomes an uncontrollable part of their daily habits.

If you wish to see yourself as you really are, the following list of questions has been prepared. Read the questions and state your answers aloud, so you can hear your own voice. This makes it easier for you to be truthful with yourself.

Self-Analysis Test Questions

- Do you complain often of "feeling badly," and if so, what is the cause?
- Do you find fault with other people at the slightest provocation?
- Do you frequently make mistakes in your work, and if so, why?
- Are you sarcastic and offensive in your conversation?
- Do you deliberately avoid associations with anyone, and if so, why?
- Do you suffer frequently with indigestion? If so, what is the cause?
- Does your life seem futile and the future hopeless? If so, why?
- Do you like your occupation? If not, why?
- Do you often feel self-pity, and if so, why?

- Are you envious of those who excel?
- Do think most of success or failure?
- Are you gaining or losing self-confidence as you grow older?
- Do you learn something of value from all mistakes?
- Are you permitting some relative or acquaintance to worry you? If so, why?
- Are you sometimes "in the clouds" and at other times in the depths of despondency?
- Who has the most inspiring influence on you? What is the cause?
- Do you tolerate negative or discouraging influences that you can avoid?
- Are you careless of your personal appearance? If so, when and why?
- Have you learned how to "drown your troubles" by being too busy to be annoyed by them?
- Would you call yourself a "spineless weakling" if you permitted others to do your thinking for you?
- Do you neglect internal bathing until you are ill-tempered and irritable?
- How many preventable disturbances annoy you, and why do you tolerate them?

- Do you resort to liquor, narcotics, or cigarettes to "quiet your nerves"? If so, will you try willpower instead?
- Does anyone "nag" you, and if so, for what reason?
- Do you have a definite major purpose, and if so, what is it, and what plan have you for achieving it?
- Are you routinely haunted by the six basic fear ghosts? If so, which ones?
- Are you consciously shielding yourself against the negative influence of others?
- Do you make deliberate choices to maintain a positive mental attitude?
- Which do you value most, your material possessions or your privilege of controlling your own thoughts?
- Are you easily influenced by others, against your own judgment?
- Has today added anything of value to your stock of knowledge or state of mind?
- Do you face squarely the circumstances that make you unhappy, or do you sidestep the responsibility?
- Do you analyze all mistakes and failures and try to profit by them, or do you take the attitude that this is not your duty?

- Can you name three of your most damaging weaknesses? What are you doing to correct them?
- Do you encourage other people to bring their worries to you for sympathy?
- Do you choose, from your daily experiences, lessons or influences that aid in your personal advancement?
- As a rule, does your presence have a negative or positive influence on other people?
- What habits of other people annoy you most?
- Do you form your own opinions or permit yourself to be influenced by other people?
- Have you created a mental state of mind to shield yourself against all discouraging influences?
- Does your occupation inspire you with faith and hope?
- Are you conscious of possessing powerful spiritual forces to keep your mind free from all forms of fear?
- Does your faith help you keep your mind positive?
- Do you feel it is your duty to share other people's worries? If so, why?
- If you believe that "birds of a feather flock together," what have you learned about yourself by studying the friends whom you attract?

- What connection, if any, do you see between the people with whom you associate most closely, and any unhappiness you may experience?
- Is it possible that someone you consider to be a friend is, in reality, your worst enemy because of the negative influence on your mind?
- By what rules do you judge who is helpful and who is damaging to you?
- Are your intimate associates mentally superior or inferior to you?
- How much time out of every 24 hours do you devote to:

  a. your occupation

  b. sleep

  c. play and relaxation

  d. acquiring useful knowledge

  e. wasting time

- Who among your acquaintances:

  a. encourages you most

  b. cautions you most

  c. discourages you most

  d. helps you most

- What is your greatest worry? Why do you tolerate it?
- When others offer you free, unsolicited advice, do you accept it without question, or analyze their motive?
- What, above all else, do you most desire? Do you intend to acquire it? Are you willing to subordinate all other desires for this one? How much time daily do you devote to acquiring it?
- Do you change your mind often? If so, why? Do you usually finish everything you begin?
- Are you easily impressed by other people's business or professional titles, college degrees, or wealth?
- Are you easily influenced by what other people think or say of you?
- Do you cater to people because of their social or financial status?
- Whom do you believe to be the greatest person living? Do you believe this person is superior to you? In what way?
- How much time have you devoted to studying and answering these questions? (At least one day is necessary for the analysis and answering the entire list.)

If you have answered all these questions truthfully, you know more about yourself than the majority of people. Study the questions carefully, return to them once each week for several months, and you will be astounded at the amount of additional knowledge of great value you will have gained by the simple method of answering the questions truthfully.

If you are not certain concerning the answers to some of the questions, seek the counsel of those who know you well, especially those who have no motive in flattering you, and see yourself through their eyes. The experience will be astonishing.

You have absolute control over only one aspect of your life—your thoughts. This is the most significant and inspiring of all known facts! Controlling your mind and thoughts reflect humanity's divine nature. This divine prerogative is the sole means by which you may control your own destiny. If you fail to control your own mind, you may be sure you will control nothing else.

You have absolute control over only one aspect of your life—your thoughts.

If you must be careless with your possessions, let it be in connection with material things. Your mind is your spiritual estate! Protect and use it with the care to which divine royalty is entitled. You were given willpower for this purpose.

Unfortunately, there is no legal protection against those who, either by design or ignorance, poison the minds of others by negative suggestion. This form of destruction should be punishable by heavy legal penalties, because it may and often does destroy someone's chances of acquiring material possessions that are protected by law.

Positive Mind Control

People with negative minds tried to convince Thomas A. Edison that he could not build a machine that would record and reproduce the human voice, "Because" they said, "no one had ever produced such a machine." Edison did not believe them. He knew that *the mind could produce anything the mind could conceive and believe,* and that knowledge is what lifted the great Edison above the common herd.

People with negative minds told F. W. Woolworth, he would go "broke" trying to run a store on five and ten cent sales. He did not believe them. He knew that he could do anything, within reason, if he backed his plans with faith. Exercising his right to keep other people's negative suggestions out of his mind, he piled up a fortune of more than a $100 million.

People with negative minds told General George Washington he could not hope to win against the vastly superior forces of the British, but he exercised his divine right to believe, therefore this book, all these years later, was published under the sovereign protection of the "Stars and Stripes"—while the name of Lord Cornwallis has been almost forgotten.

Doubting Thomases scoffed scornfully when Henry Ford tried out his first crudely built automobile on the streets of Detroit. Some said the thing never would become practical. Others said no one would pay money for such a contraption. Ford said, "I'll belt the earth with dependable motor cars." And he did! His decision to trust his own judgment piled up a fortune far greater than the next five generations of his descendants can squander.

For the benefit of those seeking vast riches, let it be remembered that practically the sole difference between Henry Ford and a majority of the people—Ford had a mind and controlled it—others have minds they don't even try to control. Now more than 150,000 men and women work for the Ford Motor Company, and there are indeed cars and trucks and SUVs worldwide.

Henry Ford has been mentioned because he is an astounding example of what a man with a mind of his own, and a will to control it, can accomplish. His record knocks the foundation from under that time-worn alibi, "I never had a chance." Ford never had a chance, either, but he created an opportunity and backed it with persistence until it made him richer than many others.

Success is achieved through self-discipline, belief in one's own vision, and the ability to control one's mind against negative influences.

Without mind control, success is not possible.

Mind control is the result of self-discipline and habit. *You either control your mind or it controls you.* There is no half-way compromise. The most practical of all methods for controlling the mind is the habit of keeping it busy with a definite purpose, backed by a definite plan. Study the record of anyone who achieves noteworthy success, and you will observe that they have control over their own mind; moreover, that they exercise that control and direct it toward the attainment of definite objectives.

Opinions

Everyone except the accurate thinker has an overabundance of opinions, and usually these are without great value. Many of them can also be dangerous and destructive when used in conjunction with personal initiative because if they are based on bias, prejudice, intolerance, ignorance, guesswork, or hearsay evidence, they may do a great deal of harm.

No opinion can be considered safe unless it is based on known facts, and no one should express an opinion on any subject without assurance that it is founded on facts, or sound hypotheses of facts. Free advice volunteered by friends and acquaintances usually is not worthy of consideration.

The accurate thinker, therefore, never acts upon such advice without giving it the closest scrutiny. Accurate thinkers permit no one to do their thinking for them. They obtain facts, information, and counsel from others, but they retain the privilege of accepting or rejecting such advice in whole, or in part.

Accurate thinkers do not form opinions based upon newspaper reports, for they cannot be sure that such information is always the result of accurate thinking. When someone says to them, "I see by the papers...," they immediately understand that the speaker has an opinion that may or may not be based on fact, and they do not allow themselves to be influenced solely by what such a person says.

– Reflection Journal –

Use the space below to capture your insights. Be honest and detailed. Writing by hand strengthens clarity and awareness.

Prompt

- Who or what drains your energy or fills your mind with doubt? How can you protect your mental environment?

My Reflections

Daily Affirmation

Speak this out loud, with conviction. Repetition builds belief, and belief transforms into action.

Affirmation for This Chapter

> ***"I surround myself with positive influences. I guard my mind and invite only thoughts that strengthen me."***

- ❑ **Repeat** it **3 times aloud.**
- ❑ **Write** it here once, slowly and deliberately:

____

____

____

____

____

____

____

____

____

____

____

Action Step

Choose one small action you can take this week to apply what you've learned.

Chapter 9

BEWARE OF "IF" EXCUSES

IF only I had spent more time analyzing my weaknesses, and less time building alibis to cover them....

People who do not succeed have one distinguishing trait in common. They know all the reasons for failure, and have what they believe to be air-tight alibis, excuses, to explain away their own lack of achievement.

Some of these alibis are clever, and a few of them are justifiable by the facts. But excuses cannot be used for money. The world wants to know only one thing—what have you achieved in life?

A character analyst complied a list of the most commonly used alibis. As you read the list, examine yourself carefully, and determine how many of these excuses, if any, are your own property, you can claim to own them. Remember, too, the philosophy presented in this book and my other books makes every one of these excuses obsolete.

IF I didn't have a wife and family...

IF I had enough "pull"...

IF I had money...

IF I had a good education...

IF I could get a job...

IF I had good health...

IF I only had time...

IF times were better...

IF other people understood me...

IF conditions around me were different...

IF I could live my life over again...

IF I did not fear what "they" would say...

IF I had been given a chance...

IF I now had a chance...

IF other people didn't "have it in for me"...

IF nothing happens to stop me...

IF I were only younger...

IF I could just do what I want...

IF I had been born rich...

IF I could meet "the right people"...

IF I had the talent that some people have...

IF I dared assert myself...

IF I only had embraced past opportunities...

IF people didn't get on my nerves...

IF I didn't have to keep house
and look after the children...

IF I could save some money...

IF the boss appreciated me...

IF I had somebody to help me...

IF my family understood me...

IF I lived in a big city...

IF I could just get started...

IF I were free to...

IF I had the personality of some people...

IF I were not so fat...

IF my talents were known...

IF I could just get a "break"...

IF I could only get out of debt...

IF I hadn't failed...

IF I knew how...

IF everybody didn't oppose me...

IF I didn't have so many worries...

IF I could marry the right person...

IF people weren't so dumb...

IF my family were not so extravagant...

IF I were sure of myself...

IF luck were not against me...

IF I had not been born under
the wrong star...

IF it were not true that "what
is to be will be"...

IF I did not have to work so hard...

IF I hadn't lost my money...

IF I lived in a different neighborhood...

IF I didn't have a "past"...

IF I only had a business of my own...

IF other people would only listen to me...

*IF (*and this is the greatest of them all*) I had the courage to see myself as I really am, I would find out what is wrong with me, and correct it. Then I might have a chance to profit from my mistakes and learn something from the experience of others. I know there is something wrong with me, or I would now be where I would have been IF I had spent more time analyzing my weaknesses, and less time building alibis to cover them.*

Building Excuses

Building excuses to explain away failure is a national pastime. The habit is as old as the human race, and is fatal to success! Why do people cling to their pet alibis? The answer is obvious. They defend their alibis because they create them! Our excuses are the children of our own imagination. It is human nature to defend our own brain-child.

Building alibis is a deeply rooted habit. Habits are difficult to break, especially when they provide justification for something we do. Greek philosopher Plato had this truth in mind when he said, "The first and best victory is to conquer self. To be conquered by self is, of all things, the most shameful and vile."

Another philosopher had the same thought in mind when he said, "It was a great surprise to me when I discovered that most of the ugliness I saw in others, was but a reflection of my own nature."

"It has always been a mystery to me," said Elbert Hubbard, "why people spend so much time deliberately fooling themselves by creating alibis to cover their weaknesses. If used differently, this same time would be sufficient to cure the weakness, then no alibis would be needed."

Generations and Beyond

Once upon a time not too long ago, a farmer, living in the mountainous section of one of the Southern states, brought home a new wife to become the stepmother of his two small boys. The wife brought with her two sons of her own, and in due time a fifth son was born of the marriage.

The home was typical of that mountain country, and the farmer was the product of four generations of his people born and reared in poverty and illiteracy.

His wife, however, came from a more prosperous section of the state and had received the benefits of a cultural background and a college education. She was not the type to accept poverty and illiteracy without protest.

The evening on which the farmer brought his new wife to their home, he introduced her to relatives and friends who had gathered there for the wedding reception. And finally he introduced her to his eldest son, a lad of nine years, with the following words:

"And now I wish you to meet the fellow who is distinguished for being the worst boy in this county and will probably start throwing rocks at you no later than tomorrow morning."

The stepmother went over to the young, so-called bad boy, placed her hand under his chin, tilted his head upward, looked him squarely in the eyes for a moment, and then turned to her husband and said, "You are wrong. This is not the worst boy in the county, but the smartest, who has not yet found the proper outlet for his enthusiasm."

Then and there began a friendship between that young boy and his new mother that was destined to project its influence for good throughout more than half of the civilized world. That was the first time anyone had ever called the boy smart. His relatives, including his father, as well as all the neighbors, had built him up in his own mind as being bad, and he had not disappointed them. His stepmother, in one brief sentence, changed all that!

Think of this story, fathers and mothers, friends and neighbors, for you have it within your power to influence your youngsters. You may be inspired to work miracles in the lives of some who need only the right influence to give them a start on the road that leads to happiness.

The stepmother was a small woman, but what she lacked in size she more than made up in ambition and enthusiasm. The week after she came into that poverty-stricken home, she held a master mind meeting with her husband that was destined to force him to part forever with poverty. At the end of the meeting it was announced that he was to enroll in a dental college. The following year, at the age of 38, he matriculated at the Louisville Dental College in Kentucky, where he remained until he was graduated.

Predicting Your Future

If you are interested in your own future, practically anyone of intelligence can help you read it quite accurately if you will answer these questions:

- First: Do you practice the habit of doing more work than you are paid for?

- Second: Do you depend on your own plans and your own efforts for advancement?
- Third: Have you trained yourself to do what ought to be done without someone telling you to do it?
- Fourth: Do you understand the principle of cause and effect?
- Fifth: Do you wait for opportunities to show up, or quietly go about creating them?

Answer these five questions correctly, and even the most elementary thinker can foretell what your finish will be.

You are living in the most advantageous age in the entire history of the world, and regardless your present station in life or how humble your beginning, the possibilities ahead of you should stagger your imagination. You are living in an age that affords every needed stimulant to arouse your imagination and inspire you with ambition.

Sow the seeds of friendly cooperation in the hearts of all whom you influence.

I am not posing as a competent judge to tell you what you ought to do, but may I suggest that you climb aboard a force that is practically irresistible—a force that will carry you on to the very summit of achievement of the highest order—if you will make it your business and your life work to sow the seeds of friendly cooperation in the hearts of all whom you influence.

Has it ever occurred to you that every failure and every mistake from which you survive, and every obstacle which you master, develop in you wisdom, strategy, and self-mastery—without which you could accomplish no great undertaking?

No one likes to meet with failure, yet every failure can be turned into a stepping-stone that will carry one to the heights of achievement, if the lessons taught by the failure are organized, classified and used as a guide.

Your failures can make for you a shield, an impenetrable protection.

If your failures embitter you toward others and develop cynicism in your heart, they will soon destroy your usefulness; but, if you accept them as necessary teachers and build them into a shield, you can make of them an impenetrable protection.

Vanity prompts us to give more thought to our triumphs than we do to our failures. Yet, if we profit by the experience of those who have accomplished most in the world, we will see that we never need to watch ourselves so closely as when we begin to attain success. Success causes a slackening of effort and a letting down of that eternal vigilance that causes us to throw the power of our combative nature into what we are doing.

A burning desire to be and to do is the starting point from which the dreamer must take off. Dreams are not born of indifference, laziness, or lack of ambition.

Our Other Selves

Remember that all who succeed in life get off to a bad start, and pass through many heartbreaking struggles before they "arrive." The turning point in the lives of those who succeed usually comes at the moment of some crisis, through which they are introduced to their "other selves."

John Bunyan wrote *The Pilgrim's Progress*, which is among the finest of all English literature, after he had been confined in prison and sorely punished because of his views on the subject of religion.

O. Henry discovered the genius that slept within his brain after he had met with great misfortune and was confined in a prison cell in Columbus, Ohio. Being forced, through misfortune, to become acquainted with his "other self" and to use his imagination, he discovered himself to be a great author instead of a miserable criminal and outcast.

Charles Dickens began by pasting labels on blacking pots. The tragedy of his first love penetrated the depths of his soul and converted him into one of the world's truly great authors. That tragedy produced, first, *David Copperfield,* then a succession of other works that made this a richer and a better world for all who read his books.

Helen Keller became deaf, dumb, and blind shortly after birth. Despite her greatest misfortune, she has written her name indelibly in the pages of the history of the great. Her entire life served as evidence that no one ever is defeated until defeat has been accepted as a reality.

Robert Burns was an illiterate country lad. He was cursed by poverty, and grew up to be a drunkard. The world was made better for his having lived, because he clothed beautiful thoughts in poetry, and thereby plucked a thorn and planted a rose in its place.

Beethoven was deaf, Milton was blind, but their names will last as long as time endures, because they dreamed and translated their dreams into organized thought.

An Open and Positive Mind

There is a difference between wishing for a thing and being ready to receive it. No one is ready for anything until the person believes it can be acquired. The state of mind must be belief, not mere hope or wish. Open-mindedness is essential for belief. Only open minds inspire faith, courage, and belief.

Remember, no more effort is required to aim high in life, to demand abundance and prosperity, than is required to accept misery and poverty.

– Reflection Journal –

Use the space below to capture your insights. Be honest and detailed. Writing by hand strengthens clarity and awareness.

Prompt

- What IF excuses do you most often use to delay action? How can you replace them with decisive steps?

My Reflections

Daily Affirmation

Speak this out loud, with conviction. Repetition builds belief, and belief transforms into action.

Affirmation for This Chapter

> ***"I take action now. I will not be held back by excuses—my future is built by the choices I make today."***

- ❑ **Repeat** it **3 times aloud.**
- ❑ **Write** it here once, slowly and deliberately:

Action Step

Choose one small action you can take this week to apply what you've learned.

CONCLUSION

As mentioned in the Preface, temporary, fleeting fear is an important and quite normal function of the human mind. The fleeting fear of being hit as we cross the street serves to make us cautious by momentarily forcing our attention on the problem of getting across safely. This type of fear teaches us attentiveness, but the fear is forgotten as soon as we have safely reached the other side.

The second important purpose of fear is to mobilize the body in defense of our life against a threatening situation. For example, you hear breaking glass near the front door when you are getting ready for bed and then you hear footsteps inside your home. The fear you feel alerts you to the possibility of physical danger and your mind immediately takes action to seek safety.

Frequently, though, fear is not a reaction to a specific danger—now it is more a learned habit of response, a pattern of thinking that defeats your quest for happiness and effective living.

We fear most the unknown. When you seek knowledge and understanding of your fears, it will be replaced by faith through a cultivated and nurtured positive mental attitude. Fears can be eradicated and exchanged for a smooth, effectively functioning mind-body-soul mindset.

You can replace ghostly, lurking fears with self-understanding and faith in yourself and the Creator. You know now that preparing yourself for a fearless lifestyle is not difficult. It begins with study, analysis, and understanding the three enemies you must clear out of your mind—*indecision, doubt,* and *fear!*

Seek knowledge and understanding of your fear, and it will be replaced by faith.

The philosophy to outwit the six ghosts of fear as a whole analyzes an unfortunate condition that has produced huge numbers of people to poverty, and it states a truth that must be understood by all who accumulate riches, whether measured in terms of money or a state of mind of far greater value than money.

This book highlighted the cause and the cure of the "ghosts" that haunt us off and on throughout our lives. Now you know the names, habits, and places where they live. Now you know how to determine which, if any, of the six common fears have attached themselves to you.

Never be deceived by the habits of these subtle ghostly enemies. Sometimes they remain hidden in the subconscious mind where they may be difficult to locate and eliminate. But *always remember that each* ***can*** *be overcome and defeated.*

Living a Fearless Life of Personal Achievement

In parting, I remind you that life is a checkerboard, and the player opposite you is *time.* If you hesitate before moving, or neglect to move promptly, your pieces will be wiped off the board by *time.* You are playing against a partner who will not tolerate indecision!

No one can get something for nothing. Everything worth having has a definite price, and that price must be paid. The rules of personal achievement are as definite as the rules of mathematics. If ever there was a true science, it is the science of personal achievement.

You are a student of this philosophy. Therefore you are deprived of alibis for failure, including the grandfather of them all, "I never had an opportunity." You have an opportunity, and it lies in the privilege of availing yourself of the combined knowledge of more than 500 men of great achievement who have made this philosophy available to you, that is shared with you within the many books I've written.

What are you going to do with your opportunity?

Success does not require a great amount of knowledge about anything, but it does call for the persistent use of whatever knowledge you may have.

- How am I using my time?
- How much time am I wasting, and why am I wasting it?
- What am I going to do to stop the waste?

These are the questions that should claim your earnest attention throughout your days.

Fearless and successful people must know themselves, not as they think they are, but as their habits have made them. Therefore, take inventory of yourself to discover where and how you are using your time.

Previously you may have had a logical excuse for not having forced life to come through with whatever you asked, but that alibi is now obsolete, because you are in possession of the powerful master key that unlocks the door to life's bountiful riches—the privilege of creating in your own mind, a burning desire for a definite form of riches.

There is no penalty for the use of the key, but there is a price you must pay if you do not use it. The price is failure. There is a reward of stupendous proportions if you put the key to use—the satisfaction that comes to all who conquer self and force life to pay whatever is asked.

The reward is worthy of your effort. Will you make the start and be convinced?

Pacemaker Instead of Ghosts

Choose as your pacemaker some prosperous, self-reliant person who is obviously successful. Make up your mind not only to catch up with that person, but to excel; but do this silently, without mentioning to anyone what you're doing.

A number of years ago, while teaching a class down in Long Beach, California, the value of a pacemaker was brought out in a very vivid lesson. It was one of those terrifically foggy nights when I could not tell where I was except in relation to the white lines painted on the highway. The lights of the car did not penetrate very far and I had to creep along.

A car was found that was equipped with fog lights and two high-candlepower spotlights that could light up the white lines for a considerable distance. This extra lighting enabled the pacemaker to travel at near normal speed.

I took advantage of his trail breaking and drove along behind him. It was evident that if he encountered any obstacles, he would give sufficient warning so that I could stop and avoid trouble.

So it is in life. If you pick out someone who is traveling the same road you have chosen, that person will light up the pitfalls for you, and thereby you may avoid some of them. Remember to carry your share of the load, however; and when you have passed your first pacemaker, assume the role for someone else.

When you select a pacemaker, be sure to choose someone who keeps moving at the same speed, or faster, than you yourself wish to travel. If the person slows down too much, or turns off on a side road, switch to another trailblazer.

A Philosopher's Creed

I offer the following for your consideration and possible adoption into your outlook of life:

- Let me be open-minded on all subjects so I may grow mentally and spiritually.
- May the time never come when I am above learning from the humblest person.
- Let me never forget that a closed mind is a narrow mind.
- May I never express opinions on any subject unless the opinions are founded on reasonable, dependable knowledge.
- Forbid that I should ever find fault with another because he or she may not agree with me.
- May I always show a wholesome respect for those with whom I may not agree.

- Let me be always mindful of the fact that all my knowledge is as nothing when compared to all that remains to be learned.
- Give me the courage to admit my ignorance when I am asked a question about which I know little or nothing.
- May I always share with others such knowledge as I may possess that can be helpful to them.
- Let me never forget that humility of heart attracts more friends than all the wisdom of humankind.
- Let me remain always a student in search of truth, and never pretend to be a finished scholar on any subject.

Throughout this book I have endeavored to introduce you to that "other self" who, once recognized, will provide all the proof you could desire when considering the past, present, and future. Which is another way of saying I induce readers to look "within" for the answer to the riddles of life—to *think* for themselves—about relationships, fear, success, joy, and all that makes an enjoyable existence.

– Reflection Journal –

Use the space below to capture your insights. Be honest and detailed. Writing by hand strengthens clarity and awareness.

Prompt

- Looking back on the six ghosts of fear, which one most often haunts you, and what is your plan to outwit it?

My Reflections

Daily Affirmation

Speak this out loud, with conviction. Repetition builds belief, and belief transforms into action.

Affirmation for This Chapter

> *"I am free from fear. I live with faith, courage, and purpose, and I outwit every ghost that tries to hold me back."*

- ❑ **Repeat** it **3 times aloud.**
- ❑ **Write** it here once, slowly and deliberately:

Action Step

Choose one small action you can take this week to apply what you've learned.

About

NAPOLEON HILL

(1883–1970)

"Remember that your real wealth can be measured not by what you have—but by what you are."

Napoleon Hill was an American self-help author best known for his groundbreaking book *Think and Grow Rich*, one of the best-selling personal development books of all time. Born in 1883 in rural Virginia, Hill began his career as a journalist before being commissioned by industrialist Andrew Carnegie to interview the most successful people of his time.

For more than 25 years, Hill studied the habits and philosophies of influential figures including Henry Ford, Thomas Edison, and Alexander Graham Bell. His work laid the foundation for modern personal success literature, emphasizing the power of desire, faith, and persistence.

Napoleon Hill's teachings continue to inspire millions worldwide to unlock their potential and pursue their dreams with purpose and determination.

For
Additional Information

about **Napoleon Hill products, please contact:**

Napoleon Hill Foundation
University of Virginia

Wise College Relations Apt. C
1 College Avenue
Wise, VA 24293

Don Green, Executive Director

Telephone: 276-328-6700
email: napoleonhill@uvawise.edu
Website: www.naphill.org

THANK YOU FOR READING THIS BOOK!

If you found any of the information helpful, please take a few minutes and leave a review on the bookselling platform of your choice.

BONUS GIFT!

Don't forget to sign up to our newsletter and grab your free personal development ebook here: